Onians, Dick
Carving the human figure

CARVING THE HUMAN FIGURE

studies in wood and stone

CARVING THE HUMAN FIGURE

studies in wood and stone

Dick Onians

GUILD OF MASTER CRAFTSMAN PUBLICATIONS LTD

First published 2001 by
Guild of Master Craftsman Publications Ltd
Castle Place, 166 High Street,
Lewes, East Sussex BN7 1XU

Edited by Stephen Haynes
Designed by Christopher Halls at Mind's Eye Design, Lewes
Cover design by Lovelock & Co
Set in Sabon

Colour origination by Viscan Graphics (Singapore)
Printed and bound by Kyodo Printing (Singapore)

For
Frances

ACKNOWLEDGEMENTS

I should like to thank the following for particular help given consciously or unwittingly to me in the preparation of this book: The City and Guilds of London Art School, my colleagues and students there and elsewhere, Dr and Mrs J. M. A. Critchley for the use of the skeleton from their student days, and Emma Lavender for the loan of her family skeleton. I am grateful to Edward Arnold (Publishers) for permission to use drawings from *Anatomy for Artists* by Eugene Wolff. Where I have known the originator, I have named the students, friends and others whose work appears here with their permission. To them I am duly grateful. I am also indebted to Heather Griffin, to Leslie Lonsdale-Cooper for her continuing guidance and advice, and to the staff of GMC Publications for their patience, courtesy and willing support – especially to Stephen Haynes for his intelligent, informed and sympathetic editing. My particular thanks go to my wife, Frances, who has encouraged me unstintingly and typed most of this book.

MEASUREMENTS

Although care has been taken to ensure that the metric measurements are true and accurate, they are only conversions from imperial; they have been rounded up or down to the nearest whole millimetre, or to the nearest convenient equivalent in cases where the imperial measurements themselves are only approximate. When following the projects, it is important to use either the metric or the imperial measurements consistently; do not mix units.

SAFETY

Woodcarving should not be a dangerous activity, provided that sensible precautions are taken to avoid unnecessary risk.

Always ensure that work is securely held in a suitable clamp or other device, and that the workplace lighting is adequate.

Keep tools sharp; blunt tools are dangerous because they require more pressure and may behave unpredictably. Store them so that you, and others, cannot touch their cutting edges accidentally.

Be particular about disposing of shavings, finishing materials, oily rags, etc., which may be a fire hazard.

Do not work when your concentration is impaired by drugs, alcohol or fatigue.

Do not remove safety guards from power tools such as angle grinders; pay attention to electrical safety.

It is not safe to use a chainsaw without the protective clothing which is specially designed for this purpose, and attendance on a recognized training course is strongly recommended. Be aware that regulations governing chainsaw use are revised from time to time.

The safety advice in this book is intended for your guidance, but cannot cover every eventuality: the safe use of hand and power tools is the responsibility of the user. If you are unhappy with a particular technique or procedure, do not use it – there is always another way.

CONTENTS

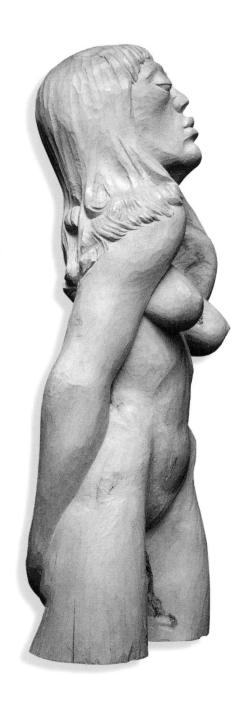

INTRODUCTION

The human figure is the most important subject in sculpture, except under Islam where making it is regarded as trespassing on the preserve of Allah. Apart from plant forms, it is probably the subject most often used.

Representations of the human form or its parts have been used for magic, for religious and secular ritual, for political ends, as aids to prayer, for support in the afterlife, as mementoes of the living, as records for posterity, as presents or as playthings. Sometimes they are a celebration of nothing more, nor less, than the maker's wonder or joy in his or her existence. Sometimes the work is only a study, a learning experience or an experiment. This book deals with the subject as a learning experience, which it is hoped will eventually give the carver the knowledge and confidence to express his or her unique ideas and feelings about the human figure.

Some representations of the figure are more effective than others, although not every culture or generation agrees on which these are. The ones that affect us most are those done with the most conviction, excitement or insight. Mere skill in sculpting a literal copy of a person is impressive but, unless the artist has put something of him- or herself into the work, it feels sterile except to a sterile or uncultivated mind. The work of cultures where technique is put above all else, as evinced in some nineteenth-century carving, fails to satisfy for this reason.

Today the opportunities for seeing sculptures from different ages and cultures are so extensive that it seems fruitless to try to improve on the most accurate sculptures of the past. Such new attempts could be accused of lack of originality and might scornfully be ranked as 'all craft and no art'. This and the current fashion for conceptual art probably explain why few art schools now teach life work except in the foundation year, the students being encouraged to be expressive and original. This is no obstacle to the lucky few with dexterity, drive and an instinctive understanding of the human form, but even in art schools there are people whose talents need to be educated. Perhaps some of their teachers, not having learnt to do it themselves, cannot pass on the ability to model or carve the human figure. Besides, modern casting methods that make it easy to take moulds from living people might be thought to have made these skills redundant.

The importance of drawing and modelling from life

The life class was the most important element in an artist's training from the Renaissance onwards. Life drawing fell out of fashion in art schools in the 1970s and '80s, but is coming back. Now the life class has an importance that it did not appear to have in the days when patrons expected sculptures to be accurate representations of nature. Then, the sculptor was learning how to copy the human form as an end in itself. Of course, unless he was being taught to draw or sculpt to a formula, the student was also learning observation and an understanding of the way things fit together in nature, particularly how internal structure affects shape on the surface. This is the great value of life study today, whether the artist is later going to work from life or not. With practice and sympathetic teaching, drawing

FIG 0.1 *Woman's head carved in lime or linden (Tilia x europaea) by Anna Twinam-Cauchi. Although at the time of carving Anna's technique was not perfected, her knowledge of the head has enabled her to make a sculpture that has great feeling and that reads well*

FIG 0.2 *Life drawing by Anna Twinam-Cauchi. The lines show that this is a study in which she has constantly made corrections as she worked both at the outlines and proportions and at the volumes of the figure. A life drawing should be a study, not a picture in its own right*

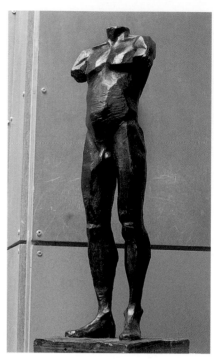

FIG 0.3 *Cement cast of a life figure by Dominic Tuck. This is a record of an examination of the main forms and masses of the standing figure. They may not all be accurate, but they are an exploration of the forms*

and modelling skills develop so that what is eventually produced is more informed than a mere 'photographic' representation and can be far more powerful. The sculptor who has mastered the figure (Fig 0.1) can concentrate on putting in and conveying the intensity of feeling that is often lacking in the work of someone who is struggling, with insufficient knowledge, to get the shape right.

Obviously, if you want to paint, model or carve the human form you need to know it. Drawing offers the quickest way to learn, as the amount recorded in a session is far more than can be put down in clay, wood or stone. But, even if you intend never to work with the human figure, the lessons of the life class are wide-reaching and cannot easily be learnt

any other way. The human has weight, and a skeleton and muscles which affect surface form and change shape with changes of position. In drawing all this you learn not only drawing technique but also the importance of underlying structure, rhythms and proportions that humans feel comfortable with and, above all, how to observe. If you do it long enough the habit of observation enriches your whole life (Figs 0.2 and 0.3).

It is, of course, quite possible to carve the human form without attending a drawing or modelling class (Fig 0.4). Millions of such sculptures have been made, many very successfully. Some obviously have been intended as symbols, and cannot have corresponded with what their makers

FIG 0.4 Diver whittled in willow (Salix alba) by Dick Onians. This very early piece shows every sign of having been done by an inexperienced carver who has seen classical sculpture in museums but has certainly done no life studies

FIG 0.5 Prophet in pear (Pyrus communis) by Dick Onians. The figure here is largely covered by drapery, but that and the face and hands are very much stylized to capture a sort of vigorous defiance

FIG 0.6 Skaters in teak (Tectona grandis) by Dick Onians. This piece is no more than an evocation of the movements of skaters, and is so far removed from the human form that it needs its title to remind the viewer of the inspiration. Perhaps it will colour people's vision of skaters in the future

The history of figure work as a model for the development of a modern artist

and contemporaries saw objectively with their eyes, but did correspond with their psychological vision. Many modern artists aim to produce work like this. However, for this we must have a strong psychological vision and a compulsion to express it. This is why the work of people with psychiatric problems has so much impact. The rest of us find it hard to don the mantle of the 'primitive' or the naïve; we have seen too many accurate figure sculptures. Inevitably, when we attempt it, our carvings tend to look wrong or ridiculous to those with an educated eye. On the other hand, many of those earlier sculptures where the sculptor has tried to get close to the actual appearance of the human shape do succeed. They are exciting because the carver was excited about doing even better than someone else, probably his master. He was pioneering in unknown territory. He was probably gifted and was always sincere.

Historically in Western art, once absolute naturalism in the figure was achieved, artists went on to express depth of emotion in the features and in extravagant poses, and to show off in tumultuous drapery and depiction of minute surface detail. After a time technical mastery palled. By the twentieth century, sculptors had turned to treating the figure as a symbol (Fig 0.5), or stylizing some visual aspect such as movement, then, tiring of that, to abstract sculpture in which the viewer has difficulty in seeing anything recognizably human (Fig 0.6). For an artist each phase is good only as long as the excitement of discovery and invention lasts.

If you are reading this, it is because you are interested in learning how to carve the figure and are prepared to take the trouble to master it so that you can go safely towards putting feeling into naturalism, or towards symbolism and stylization. Except for a very few lucky people who are able instinctively to draw and model successfully, an understanding of technique and of the structures of the human body has to be taught.

Learning to look at the figure

This book is a guide to the features of the human figure that should be noticed. For, paradoxically, although we inhabit human bodies and probably spend much time looking at them, we generally have little knowledge of the shapes and their causes unless someone points them out.

There are many good anatomy books for artists, and I suggest that you use one (some are listed on page 162). However, they do not specifically draw attention to the features of most importance to the carver. I therefore begin with a chapter on the anatomy of the whole figure. In some chapters I spend some time on modelling the anatomy in order to encourage the habits of thinking of the underlying structure and of making maquettes in clay. However, anatomy study should be used only to complement that most useful preparation: doing masses of drawing and modelling from life. In this way you learn how the anatomy affects the surface form, and gain sufficient knowledge to model and carve figures with different proportions in a wide range of postures.

Five chapters deal with carving various parts of the body, two of which – the head and the hand – have frequently been represented on their own. The torso, being a solid mass, has often survived, particularly in stone sculpture, when the rest has been damaged; this has led to its also being treated as a valid subject for sculpture. The whole figure,

both male and female, is also shown, nude and clothed. Whether you use classical drapery or modern dress, the underlying anatomy has an important impact on its shapes. Besides, the shapes of clothing can themselves be exploited to produce powerful effects.

Respecting the differences between the natural body and the carving material

When you carve the figure in any material, you represent bone, flesh and hair with something that is quite different in appearance and behaviour. Furthermore, to attempt to include every detail is not only so boring – and impossible – for the carver as to rob the carving of any life, but can also distract the viewer from seeing the aspects the carver is consciously, and unconsciously, interested in. Because you are working in three dimensions your principal concern is with the volumes, masses and lines of your sculpture – sculptural form – not with the surfaces. Therefore, although the purpose of these exercises is to teach the appearance of the figure and some processes for carving it, I am also concerned with showing it as sculpture. A sculpture should respect the material and have some design, feeling or insight of the maker in it. It should also read well from a distance. The first time you carve any of the subjects shown here, your work may fall short of these goals and look like only a study. However, your later carvings, being more confident, are bound to have more of you in them, and to have strength and authority.

When you have made your first careful studies directly from life and are in better command of your subject and material, you will have the freedom to experiment with simplifying the forms. I have therefore included a chapter on stylizing the figure.

This book does not give recipes for carving the figure. I fervently believe that the best work is done when the carver is thinking for him- or herself.

If you are a newcomer to woodcarving, I advise you to gain at least basic carving skills before tackling this difficult subject. My previous book, *Essential Woodcarving Techniques* (GMC Publications, 1997), deals particularly with technique. In the present book, I therefore describe the technique only where it seems appropriate. I recommend the sculptor's approach rather than that of the traditional carver, in that the sculptor tends to work around forms rather than always going the way the grain may suggest. This approach helps the carver to avoid the square figures and superficial treatment often seen in the work of the inexperienced.

Carving figures in relief is far more difficult than many new carvers realize, but as many carvers wish to attempt pictorial art, and since relief carving allows compositions that would be too fragile in the round, I devote a chapter to this subject.

Although stone is carved with different tools and techniques and does not allow such long, slender forms, the ways of looking at the figure are the same. I therefore hope that this book will be of interest to stone carvers, too.

When confronted with the plethora of anatomical details and names, it is comforting to know that you can carve just as good a figure without having memorized them all. I have included so many mainly for ease of reference, but also to satisfy your intellectual curiosity and because it seemed unfair to omit some. I have, however, left it to you to find out much about the hand and arm muscles.

There are many women carvers, but for the sake of brevity I use hereafter the convention of writing 'he' instead of 'he or she' throughout.

While I claim no originality for the studies of the naturalistic form (except where there is obvious original design, as in the drapery and relief panels), there is copyright on the stylized examples, as they are definitely the original creations of their carvers – and please remember that the illustrations themselves may not be reproduced without permission.

Much of the material in this book has already appeared as articles in *Woodcarving* magazine, and I refer also to examples shown in my book *Essential Woodcarving Techniques*. Note that the carved examples in the following chapters are my own work except where otherwise stated.

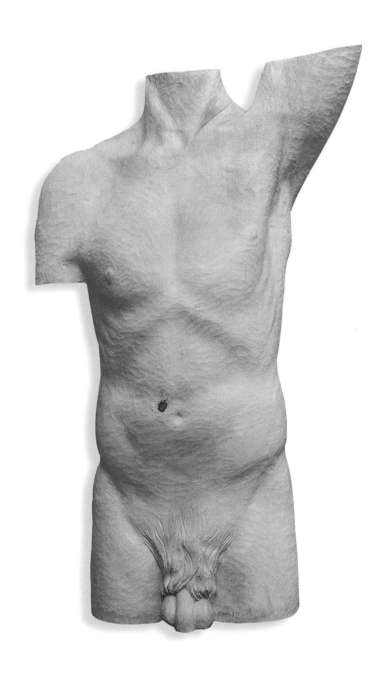

BASIC HUMAN ANATOMY

There are several excellent books on anatomy for artists, and others which are not so helpful. Some are done with the painter in mind, and lack depth in the drawing or photography. They may be beautifully drawn, but if you cannot tell whether forms recede or advance, and what the volume of a form is, it is better to seek more intelligible illustrations. This chapter is intended to point out the aspects of anatomy which are important for a sculptor. It cannot give all the information you will need, so I recommend you seek out a good textbook that is free of the above faults. All those listed on page 162 are good, but especially Wolff's and Goldfinger's books.

We are all aware that people even of the same racial type have individual features. Therefore, any remarks made in this and subsequent chapters about particular shapes and proportions of the human anatomy must be seen as generalizations unless otherwise stated.

The first and most fundamental aspect of anatomy is the skeleton (Figs 1.1 and 1.2). Even if you cannot see it – because it is covered by flesh or, more thoroughly, by clothes – it is always there, and inevitably affects the outer appearance. Bones may be jointed and be able to form angles,

flesh may make them appear rounded, but still each bone is rigid and does not naturally change shape. If you learn the basic bones, the ones which most obviously affect surface shape, you will avoid making arms and legs bent like bananas, fingers as smooth as sausages, and torsos and heads like rectangular boxes.

The skull

Starting from the top, the skull is not a sphere, nor is the face flat with lumps and holes on its surface. One of the most telling views in sculpture is from above. If the sculpture works well all round, it is because there is no clear border between front, sides and back. One is also more likely to get good depth in the modelling of forms if one observes the top view. The top view of the skull shows that it is like an egg with the little end at the front and the big end at the back, slightly flattened (Fig 1.3). The widest part is usually just above and behind the ear hole or **external auditory meatus**, which is situated immediately in front of the **mastoid**, a **process** or solid prong of bone at the bottom edge of the skull, just behind the lower jaw (Fig 1.4). (Note that words printed in bold type in the text are defined in the Glossary on pages 159–61.)

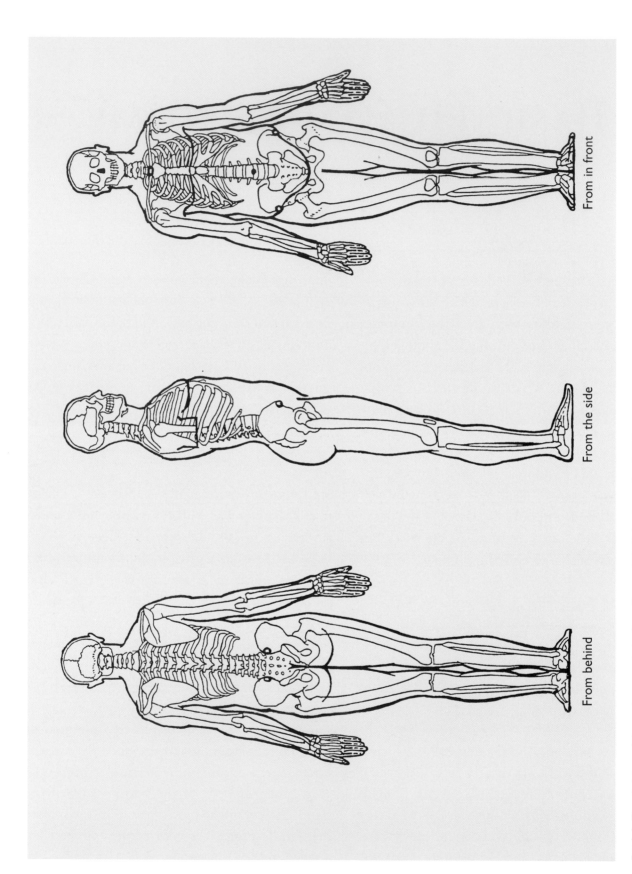

From in front

From the side

From behind

FIG 1.1 *The skeleton of the male as a whole, from Eugene Wolff,* Anatomy for Artists *(London: H. K. Lewis, 1962), by kind permission of Edward Arnold (publishers)*

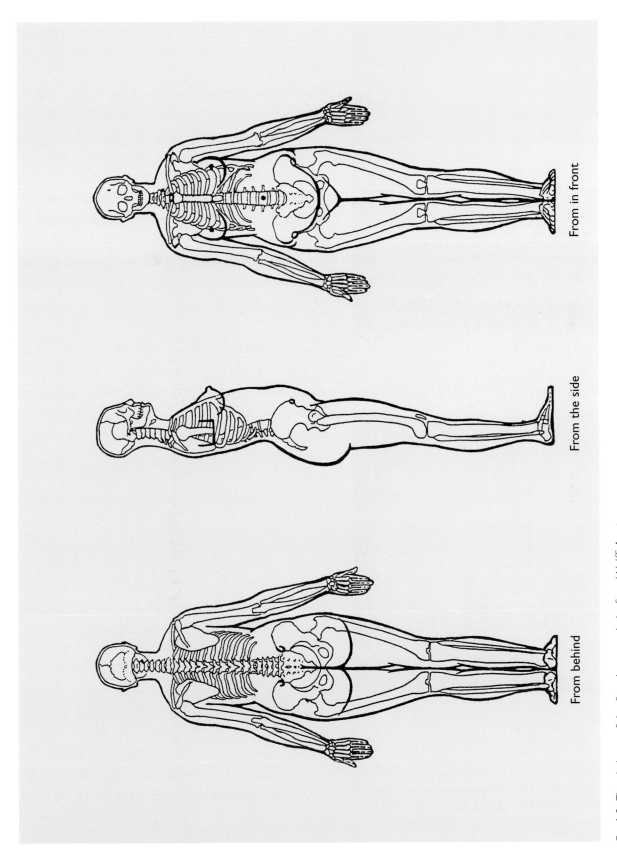

From in front

From the side

From behind

Fig 1.2 The skeleton of the female as a whole, from Wolff, Anatomy for Artists, by kind permission of Edward Arnold (publishers)

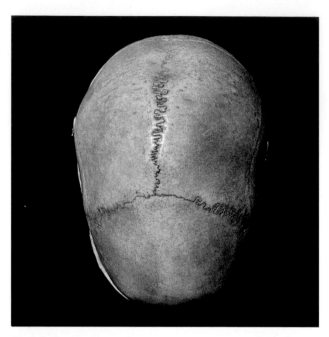

FIG 1.3 The skull seen from above, showing the shape tapering to the forehead (at the bottom of the photograph) and major sutures where the plates of bone have joined

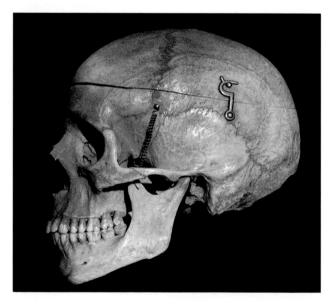

*FIG 1.4 Side view of the skull. The top has been sawn off so that medical students can study the inside of the cranium, and there is a spring attached to the front of the **ramus** of the lower jaw to imitate the action of the temporal muscle which runs from that point, through the **zygomatic arch** up onto the side of the skull. The ear hole is just behind the hinge of the lower jaw and in front of the mastoid process. Note how far the **occiput** or occipital protuberance — the hindmost part of the skull — projects behind the mastoid*

An inspection of the majority of heads done by uninitiated sculptors shows a conviction that the face seen from the side runs from the tip of the nose to the back of the eye socket, which has no more depth than a pair of spectacles. Contrary to this popular interpretation, the face of an adult takes up not one eighth of the distance between the tip of the nose and the back of the skull, but almost one third. Nevertheless, the **cranium** is by far the largest part of the human head and its shape should always be modelled or carved, or at least allowed for, from the beginning. Unless there is an elaborate hairstyle, the hair follows the shape of the skull and the ears.

Looking down from above, we see how the skull tends to flatten out across the line of the eyebrows, and that the **zygomatic arches** (the thin bars of bone that run back from the cheekbones at the bottom outside corners of the eye sockets to just in front of the ear holes) are wider than the temples. Looking up from under the chin, we see how prominent the upper and lower sets of teeth are (Figs 1.5 and 1.6). The dentist will show you casts of them which make this point strongly. We can also see how narrow the chin is, and how the two halves of the lower jaw form a V which is usually slightly narrower at the back than the zygomatic arches directly above.

Another important feature is an imaginary line drawn through the middle of the eyes. On an adult with teeth, this line is about halfway between the top of the crown (the skull's highest point) and the chin when the face is looking straight ahead. A child's jaw develops slowly, so for years there is more head above the eyes than there is below. A toothless older person also has more above the eyes than below.

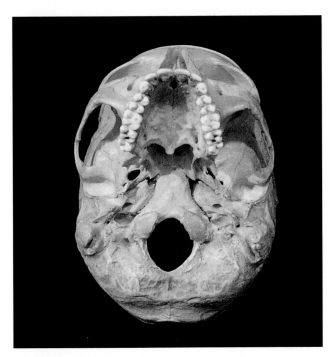

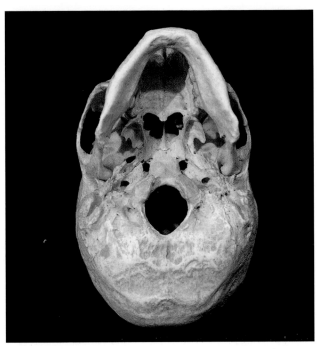

FIG 1.5 *The skull seen from below, with the lower jaw removed to show the hoop-like shape of the upper jaw. The outside corners of the eyes and the backwards slope of the cheekbones can be clearly seen*

FIG 1.6 *The skull seen from below, with the lower jaw in place. The jaw is much more pointed than many people realize*

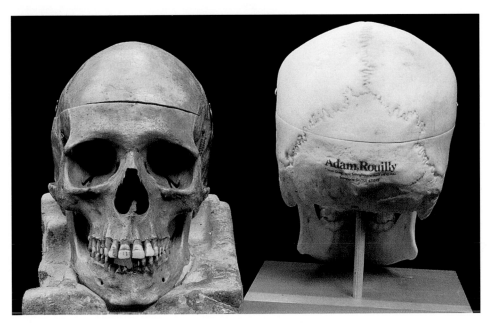

FIG 1.7 *The skull from in front and behind. The narrowness of the temples and the width of the cheekbones, especially the zygomatic arch, are clearly seen. The shape of the brow ridge and the way the surface of the bone seems to twist from the top of the brow on the outside to the underside of the brow beside the nose is also visible. The straightish sides of the back view and the flatter arc to the top of the back of the cranium are noticeable*

Many heads go wrong because the sculptor has failed to give full depth to the mouth and the eyes. The eye socket is slightly angled, so that the outside of the front of the eye **orbit** is considerably behind the bridge of the nose. Another significant feature of the eye socket is the little notch in the middle of the top, which is visible in Fig 1.7. This **supraorbital notch** is one of the pressure points which can be massaged with a fingernail to help dispel certain types of headache. Between this notch and the bridge of the nose, the bone faces increasingly downwards. Outside the notch there is a more or less pronounced ledge on top of the eye socket. It is as if there were a narrow ribbon that twists across from above the eye at the outside to below the brow towards the nose. The hair of the eyebrow tends to follow this twist.

The spinal column

The head is attached by bone to the rest of the body through the **spinal column** or backbone. Seen from in front, this should present a straight line in the upright body, but from the side it is full of curves (Fig 1.8). It is more or less rigid where it supports the ribs, with a slight forward curve which increases at the nape of the neck. It then swings back upright to join the middle of the skull at the **atlas** joint. Below the ribcage it reverses the curve to sweep back to the top of the pelvis, which is attached just below the **lumbar region**. Like the neck, this part of the backbone can move sideways and forward, and can also twist. The part of the backbone attached to the pelvis is the **sacrum**, which consists of five **vertebrae** fused together. At the lower end of this is the **coccyx**, our vestigial tail, which tucks forward again between the cleft of the buttocks.

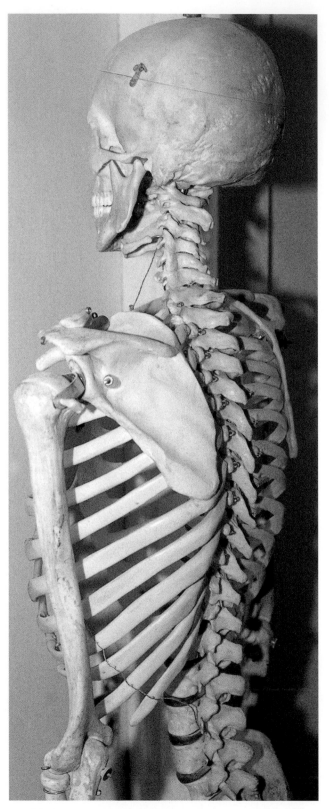

FIG 1.8 A partial side view of the ribcage, showing the curves of the spinal column

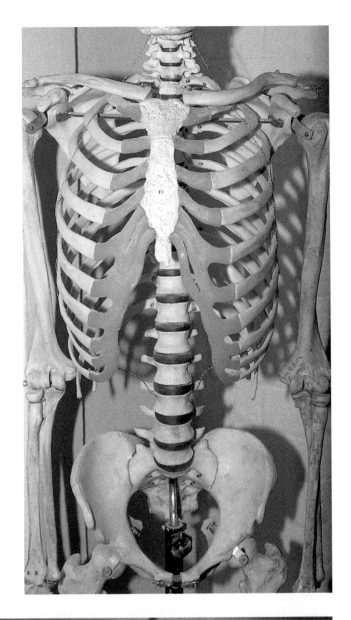

FIG 1.9 Front view of the upper part of the body, showing the cup of the pelvis, the ribcage sloping in towards the neck, the length of the neck, and the shoulder girdle

The ribcage

The ribcage or **thorax** is roughly egg-shaped, with the little end cut off at shoulder height and the bottom end flattened, with an inverted V at the front (Fig 1.9). It is not at all square. It is virtually rigid, except that the lower ribs at the front move forwards and upwards as we breathe in correctly at the bottom of our lungs, and downwards and inwards when we breathe out. The arms are attached to the thorax by muscle and ligament.

The collarbones and shoulder blades

The collarbones or **clavicles** are joined to the **sternum** at the top of the ribcage at the front, and they and the shoulder blades (**scapulae**) meet around the top end or head of the upper arm bone (**humerus**). They float around the ribcage so there is plenty of movement for the arm (Fig 1.10). Collarbones, which help in grasping and climbing, are peculiar to man and the other primates.

*FIG 1.10 Top view of the shoulder girdle. The clavicles curve back towards the shoulder and then come forward again at their outer ends, while the **coracoid process** and the **acromion** process on the end of the spine of the scapula come forward around the head of the humerus. This causes the front of the shoulder to stand forward of the chest at that point. On the back, the spine of the scapula sticks out some distance away from the spinal column and slopes forwards to the shoulder*

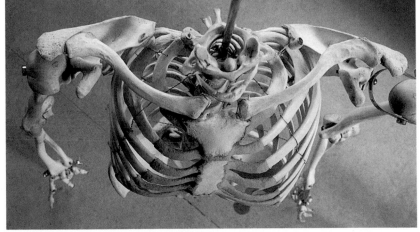

The pelvis

It is helpful to think of the head, the ribcage and the pelvis as rectangular solids when arranging a composition. This is a simplification that can be built on as the subtleties of the actual shapes are explored. The pelvis in fact is more like a cup which has the front side cut away (see Fig 1.9). Because the woman's pelvis serves to hold the baby in the womb and to allow for its passage into the open air, her pelvic bones are wider and slightly different from a man's. This actually means that the outer heads (**great trochanters**) of the thighbones (**femurs**) stick out further than the **anterior iliac crest** when viewed from the front. (The iliac crest is the top rim of the pelvis, and 'anterior' indicates the part that is towards the front.) The important thing to remember about the thorax and pelvis is that these bony structures are more or less rigid, so that each tilts as a solid object. Any irregularity in appearance is caused by the reaction of muscle and flesh, and is subordinate to the shapes of the bones.

The arms, legs, hands and feet

Arms and legs, hands and feet have similar bone structures. One long bone joins each to the body by a joint which allows the limb to move backwards and forwards or sideways. Further out there is a pair of bones, one major and one minor, which rotate around each other. The lower or fore arm is able to rotate through 180 degrees. The knee joint allows only slight rotation; for the foot to turn much to the left or right, the whole leg must rotate at the hip. The pairs of bones below the elbow and the knee both produce bumps at the surface at their lower ends (Figs 1.11 and 1.12). The more obvious wristbone is that at the

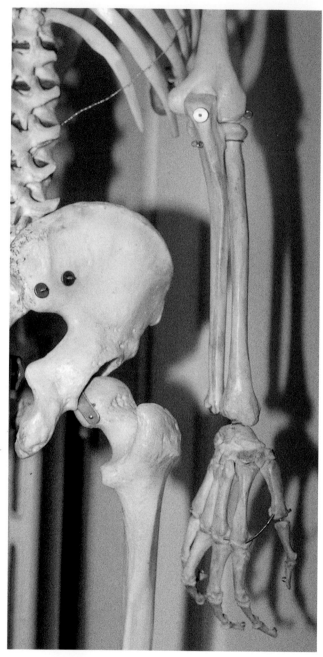

FIG 1.11 *The right lower arm bones and the hip joint from behind. The great trochanter is the knob at the head of the femur that is closest to the wrist. The swellings at the wrist ends of the* **radius** *and* **ulna***, the two lower arm bones, can be clearly seen, and are noticeable on the living person*

back of the wrist, on the side of the little finger. The prominences (**malleoli**) at the bottom ends of the lower leg bones, which we usually call the anklebones, are both very noticeable. At the

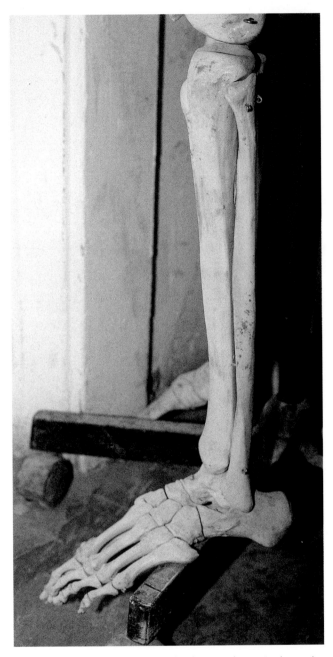

FIG 1.12 The left leg from the side, showing the major bone, the **tibia***, in front and the* **fibula** *behind. The outer* **malleolus***, or outer anklebone, can be seen at the bottom end of the fibula*

bones closely connected to form the palm of the hand and the foot from heel to sole. Every finger and toe is made up of three bones in a string, except the thumbs and big toes, which have only two bones each.

The covering of the skeleton

It is not enough to say that the body is covered with flesh. Where there is no bone, such as in the eye sockets and between pelvis and ribcage, there are organs which need protection and support. The eyeballs, whose ball-like appearance is important to the sculptor, fill the eye sockets, but the liver, stomach and intestines are hidden behind walls of muscle, possibly covered with a layer of fat. The genital organs are partly held inside the pelvis, but the female mammary glands and the male testicles and penis are planted on top of the bone structure.

The muscles

To enable the body to move there are many muscles. Like the internal organs, most are of no significance for the sculptor; but there are some very obvious superficial ones which have their own effect on surface form, both at rest and in use (Figs 1.13–1.16). Muscles operate by relaxing or contracting. When contracted, the muscle continues to have the same volume but swells sideways; the biceps are an obvious place to observe this. The Latin word *musculus* originally meant 'little mouse', because the Romans thought that muscles moved like mice under the skin. (I am indebted to my brother, John Onians, for this derivation.) It is therefore important to notice how muscles change shape as the body changes posture, or as new tasks are performed (the carving of legs in Chapter 4 is a good example of this).

elbow, the outside of the joint is protected by what we call the 'funny bone' (the **olecranon**), a development of the larger of the lower pair of bones, the **ulna**. The angle of the knee is protected in front by a moveable lump of bone, the kneecap (**patella**). Both hands and feet have many small

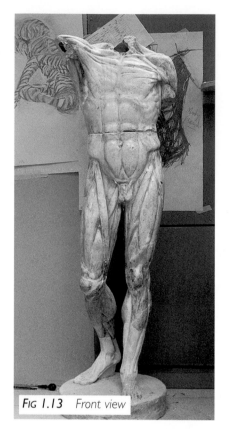

FIG 1.13 *Front view*

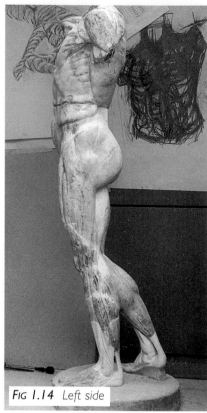

FIG 1.14 *Left side*

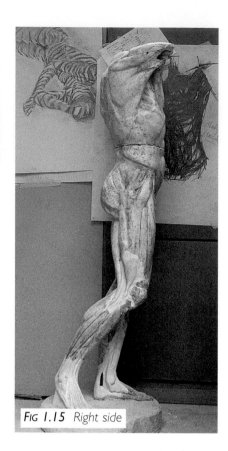

FIG 1.15 *Right side*

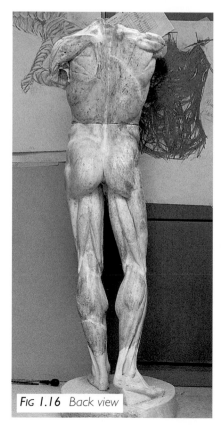

FIG 1.16 *Back view*

The 'flayed' man used to be a common feature in art schools. This much restored example is often in use at the City and Guilds of London Art School, where students use it as an aid to understanding the life figure

Fat

It may seem unkind to draw attention to the reserve of fat on the body, but it is a necessary part of us. It is true that some have more than others. Women by nature tend to have more than men; they certainly have a different distribution of fat (Figs 1.17–1.19). Fat tends to smooth out the surface form, making it less angular. Its presence on the face of a child or a young woman makes the forms very subtle and hard to capture. Where muscle attaches to bone, the bone may be prominent or may be sunk in a dip. Fat tends to form dimples over these places; the arm of a baby is a good place to see this effect.

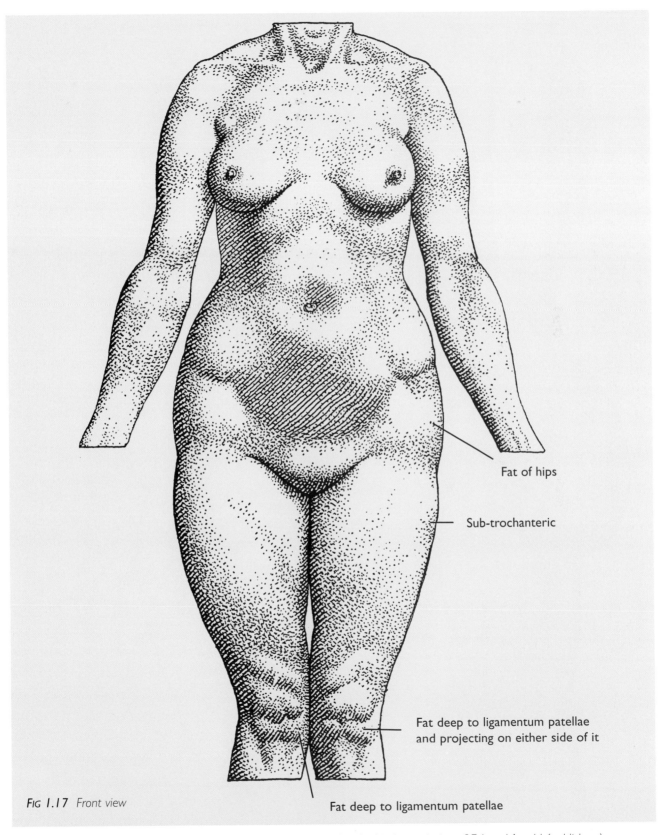

Fat of hips

Sub-trochanteric

Fat deep to ligamentum patellae
and projecting on either side of it

FIG 1.17 *Front view*

Fat deep to ligamentum patellae

The distribution of fat on a woman, from Wolff, Anatomy for Artists, *by kind permission of Edward Arnold (publishers)*

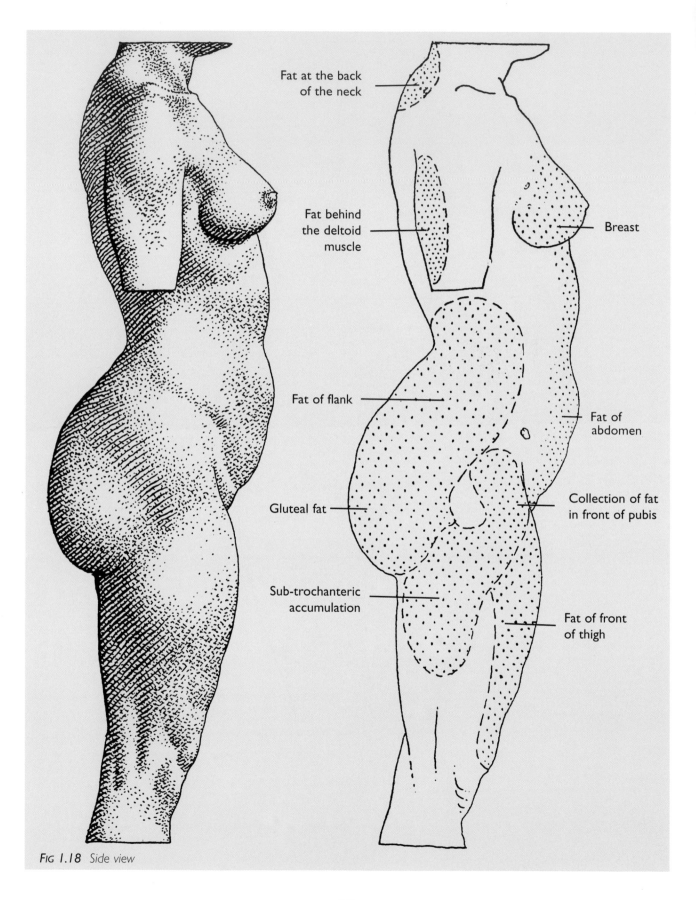

Fat at the back
of the neck

Fat behind
the deltoid
muscle

Fat of flank

Gluteal fat

Sub-trochanteric
accumulation

Breast

Fat of
abdomen

Collection of fat
in front of pubis

Fat of front
of thigh

FIG 1.18 *Side view*

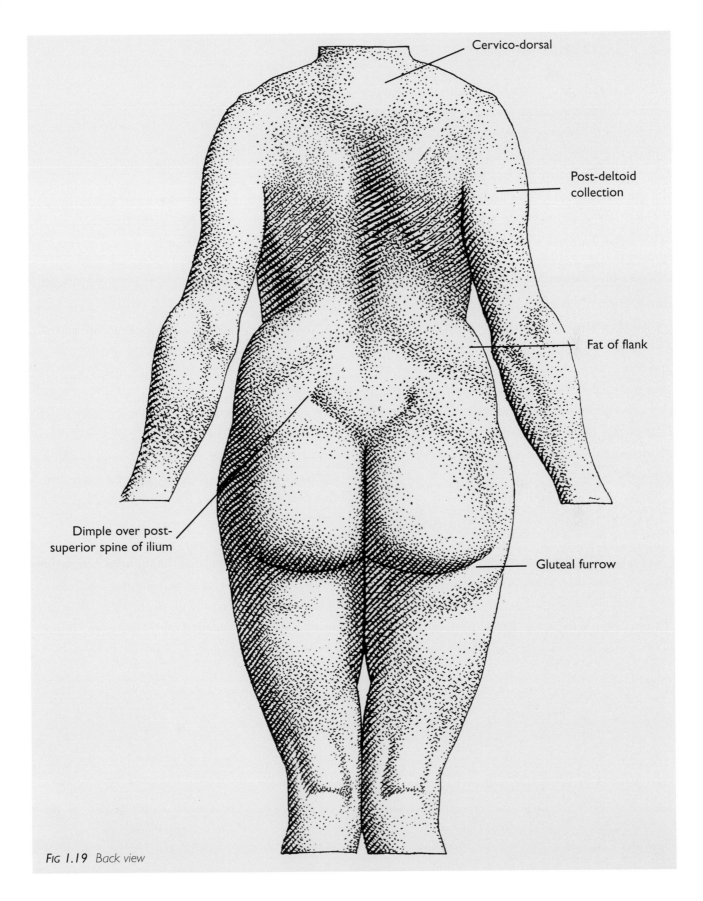

Cervico-dorsal

Post-deltoid
collection

Fat of flank

Dimple over post-
superior spine of ilium

Gluteal furrow

FIG 1.19 *Back view*

Racial differences

Different races have slightly different appearances because of differences in bone proportions and fat distribution. The eyes of people from the region of China, the so-called Mongolic races, have a fold of skin that pulls across the inside corner of the eye, the **epicanthal fold**. The races of Africa and the Far East have short, broad noses and distinctive jaw shapes; they sometimes refer to Europeans as 'long noses'. Some peoples of southern Africa have a different pelvic shape and a different distribution of fat over the hips and buttocks; this so-called **steatopygy** apparently gives them greater endurance in times of famine. Hair distribution and type varies with the races. Hair and skin colour are also peculiar to races from different parts of the world. For a carver, colour is of less importance than shape, but may affect the choice of wood colour if the carving is to be neither painted nor stained.

Growing up and ageing

Children differ considerably from adults, and their proportions change throughout childhood and adolescence (Fig 1.20). As already mentioned, the chin of a baby is far shorter than an adult's.

The nose also is undeveloped. Cheeks tend to be fatter. The arms and legs of a baby are short in comparison, and tend to be plump and rounded, often showing dimples on elbows and deep creases at wrists, knees and ankles where bone is prominent at later ages.

The development of boys and girls is also different. Girls tend to be larger than boys of the same age until about the early teens. The shape of girls, too, changes very dramatically during adolescence. The physique of boys and girls before puberty is similar, with flat chests and comparatively slim hips. For girls at puberty the breasts develop and the hips begin to widen as the distribution of fat on the hips changes.

Old age also takes its toll, with more lines on the face, sagging flesh, reduced muscle sizes and a more visible bone structure. If the teeth are lost and not replaced, the mouth sinks in and the chin moves closer to the nose. Hair loss is also more likely.

This is only a brief survey which is intended to draw attention to some of the main considerations for the sculptor of the human figure. The relevant bones and muscles will be dealt with in greater detail as each part of the body is examined in turn.

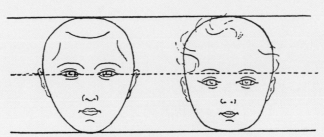

The centre line of the adult head passes through the inner angle of the eye, while in the baby it passes well above this point because of the smaller size of the skeleton of the face compared with that of the cranium

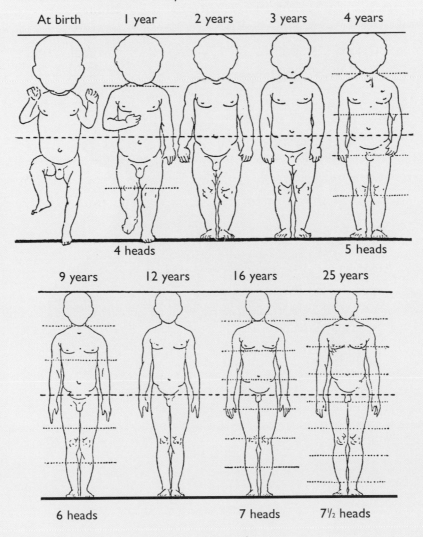

FIG 1.20 The development of the proportions of the body from infancy to adulthood, from Wolff, Anatomy for Artists, *by kind permission of Edward Arnold (publishers)*

21

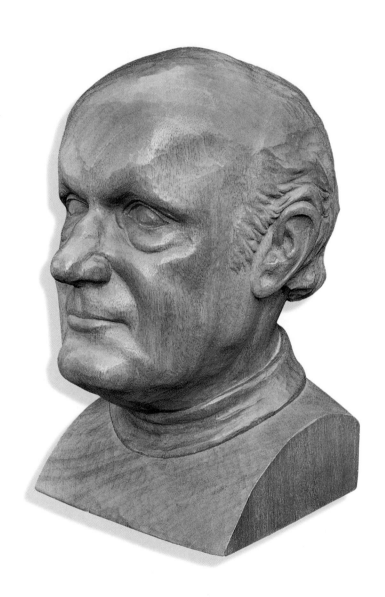

THE HEAD

The head, in particular the face, is the part of the human form most often portrayed. But, although we are probably more familiar with the human head than with anything else, carvers often fail when representing it. The length of this chapter reflects the importance of this subject; it contains lessons that are relevant to carving the rest of the figure.

The main reasons for poor head carving are that the shape of the skull and the position of the face on the head are not understood. The face is not just the brow, eyes, nose, cheeks, mouth and chin. The way we learn language is possibly responsible for this limited view. Does the face end at the ears? Where does the forehead end on a bald head?

A revealing and instructive exercise is to model the human skull in clay and then, with the aid of an anatomy book for artists, add the muscles, nose cartilage, eyeballs and ears. This achieves two ends – three, if the sculptor has not worked with clay before. The obvious benefit is that the reasons for the shape of the head become clear and the relationships between one part and another are learned. The second main benefit is that the student is encouraged to think of the underlying structure, a habit of mind needed whatever you sculpt.

Ceramic artists and potters are the only people who use clay for its own sake. Sculptors who cast things in bronze, resin, cement or plaster, and carvers, who use it to prepare designs, are both using clay as a tool. The modeller in clay, however, uses it instinctively and thinks in the opposite way to the carver. The carver works from the outside in, and the modeller builds outwards. It is a good discipline for a carver to add small pieces of clay, rather than add too much and then cut it away. It is part of the process of learning the underlying structure. Besides, cutting lumps off a clay model can distort it.

Basic equipment for clay modelling

You need only a few modelling tools (Fig 2.1). Wooden ones, preferably in boxwood (*Buxus sempervirens*), are better than plastic. Steel plaster-modelling tools are useful, too. You will also need a pair of callipers. Those illustrated in Fig 2.2 are of aluminium, 12in (305mm) long. They can be used for both inside and outside measurements, and are reasonably stiff. You can make your own in metal, wood or plastic. A spring washer and a wing nut make them easily adjustable.

The clay I used for this exercise is a slightly grogged terracotta (that is, one that is mixed with

FIG 2.1 On the left are three steel tools for plaster modelling; next is an assortment of seven home-made and shop-bought boxwood tools, with a large, heavy block for initial shaping on the right. Below are three wire modelling tools for quickly cutting away clay

powdered fired clay), but most clays will do. A potters' or sculptors' suppliers can advise you. I used about 17½lb (8kg) for the head shown in this chapter, which is life size. You will need some sort of frame or armature to support the clay. I used ³⁄₁₆in (4.5mm) square aluminium armature wire. This bends easily and keeps its shape. You will need a piece 2–3ft (600–900mm) long, and some staples.

The supporting post or peg (Fig 2.3) is a batten 1 x 1½in (25 x 38mm), about 14in (350mm) long, set into a piece of 10in (255mm) square board, 1½in (38mm) thick. The joint needs to be tight, as the weight of the clay can pull the post over, and in any case a loose peg would be awkward to work with. If the base is any thinner, you will

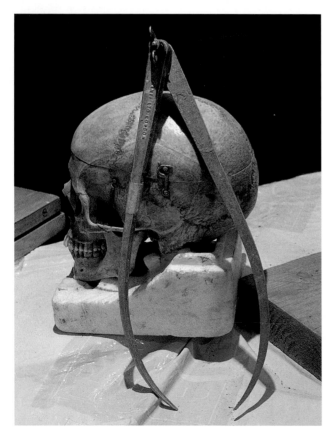

FIG 2.2 Aluminium callipers. The legs can be crossed over if necessary to take inside measurements

FIG 2.3 Beginning the armature of the head: the modelling peg is set into a stout base

need brackets to hold the post steady. The post should not be more than 1½in (38mm) square; a thicker post will hinder you if you intend to make the neck.

Real skulls are expensive and not easy to come by. Ask around – you may be able to borrow one. Some doctors keep theirs from their student days, but a good plastic replica will also work well. At the time of writing, replica skulls are available from Adam Rouilly, Crown Quay Lane, Sittingbourne, Kent, ME10 3JG (tel. 01795 471378).

Preparation

When stapling the armature wire onto the post, make sure the shape is going to fit well inside the skull's dimensions. If the wire is at or near the surface of the clay it will be a constant annoyance. The loop fastened below the spherical shape (Fig. 2.4) is to support the chin. You might also fix a bar across to take the shoulders, but I prefer to leave this for the time being, to see where I want them to be once I have modelled the head. Fill the core of the armature with wet rags, newspaper, plastic bags or polystyrene; this will save weight and clay, and also give a solid grip for the clay.

Because clay cracks and falls apart when it is dry, it has to be kept damp. A small garden hand spray and a sheet of plastic to cover the model while you are not working on it are essential. If you have no spray, you could dribble water onto it from a detergent bottle or a sponge. Cover it with a damp cloth before sealing it with plastic, to keep it damp for longer. To prevent the growth of hair-like fungus, put disinfectant in the water.

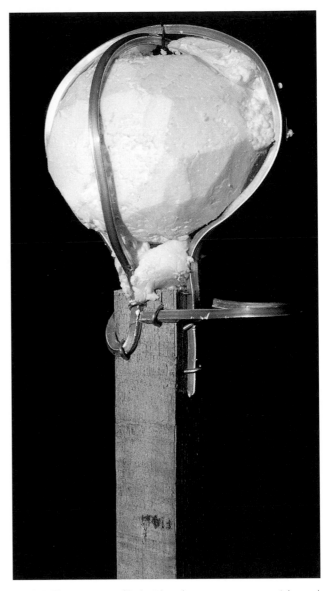

FIG 2.4 *The armature filled with polystyrene, to save weight and to provide a key for the clay. A loop of armature wire has been fastened at jaw level to support the lower part of the face*

The cranium

If you did not have a skull (cranium) you would not have a face. It is the most important part of the structure of the head, so you should start from the back of the skull by taking a large handful of clay, pushing it up under the skull and working it around the back end, the occiput. A large piece of

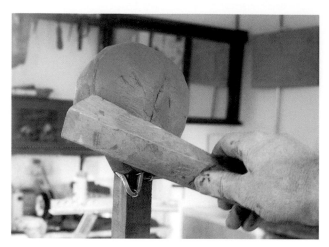

FIG 2.5 *A large modelling tool gives strong, simple forms*

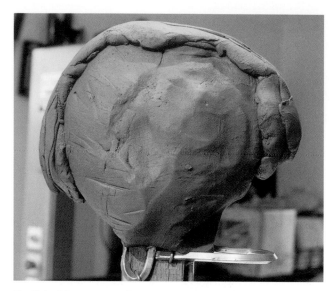

FIG 2.6 *After a core of clay has been pressed on, profiles of the cranium can be built up and filled in*

wood can be used to bash it into shape (Fig 2.5). If the wood has a rough texture it will matt the surface, which makes it easier to see the shape. You will notice I have not tried to conceal the effects of the modelling tools. It is important you are not sidetracked into dealing with surface details. A smooth, shiny surface, on a clay model as on a carving, stops the eye at the surface and makes it hard to read the form.

Once you have made a good round core of clay over the armature, you can use the callipers to take measurements from your reference skull, from the forehead to the back of occiput, and across the widest part (about one third of the distance forward from the back). Add blobs of clay fore and aft and at the sides to meet these dimensions, then fill in, remembering that the crown – the highest point – is usually nearer the back than the front (Fig 2.6). Seen from above, the skull is rather like an egg, with the forehead at the little end, as we saw in Fig 1.3. By holding your model up in front of the skull, or the skull in front of your model, you can check one silhouette against the other. Keep using the biggest modelling tool you can, to keep the forms broad and simple.

The cranium is often flatter on the back of the crown than in front of it. The **sutures** (literally 'stitching') where the bones knitted in infancy can sometimes mark changes in shape. The skull I used had quite a sharp ridge along the suture that ran along the crown. The barely worn teeth and the clear sutures suggested the skull was from a young person, probably female because of the small ridges of bone on the eyebrows and the prong of bone sticking forward at the bottom of the nose cavity. Sutures become blurred on an older skull.

Another useful marker is the slight line or ridge of bone (visible in Fig 2.7) which runs from the top of the eye socket up and around the side of the skull to curve down and forward to the mastoid process, the lump of bone just below and behind the ear hole. This ridge marks the border of the huge temporal muscle. While shaping the cranium, keep the centre of the weight of the clay slightly behind the pole; the weight of the face will later balance it.

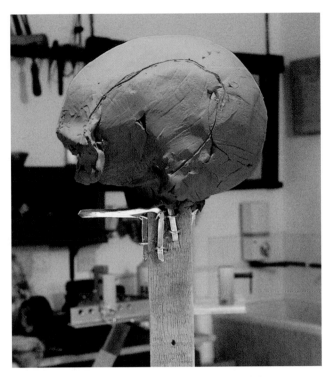

FIG 2.7 *The face should not be attempted until the cranium is ready to receive it. Here the eye sockets are just begun, with the brow and the outside of the orbit. The line scratched on the side of the skull marks the boundary of the temporal muscle which will be applied later. It is usually visible on the bone, and is a useful reference point*

FIG 2.8 *The bone structure is complete. The modelling tool shows how much further back the outside of the eye socket is than the inside corner of the eye*

Eyes and cheekbone

Once the cranium is shaped, start on the eye sockets (Fig 2.7). Notice how much further they project sideways than the forehead. Many sculptors and carvers do not realize how far back the outside of the socket is. You can see for yourself how the eye is set in the head by looking straight ahead while you stretch both arms out to your sides. See how far back your hands can go before you lose sight of your fingers out of the corners of your eyes. This ability to see forwards and sideways simultaneously is partly because the eye is a ball, and partly because the side of the eye orbit between the temple and the cheekbone is curved backwards (Fig 2.8).

When beginning the eye socket, look for the small notch in the middle at the top, the supraorbital notch (see page 12 and Fig 1.7). Towards the nose the bone is turned downwards. Towards the temple it is as if the surface of the inside of the socket twists across the notch, and ends up facing upward on the outside half of the brow, giving rise to a flattened area.

Observe the relationship between the eye socket and the nose and cheekbones. The bone of the nose is surprisingly small. The eye orbit sweeps up onto it from below. The large lump of bone just at the bottom outside corner of the eye is the cheekbone proper. The thin strip of bone curving out and back from the bottom corner of the orbit to meet the skull again just above the ear hole is the zygomatic arch. Because it is so thin and sticks out so far from the skull, you will probably need to support it with clay as I did. The zygomatic arch must curve outwards from the cheekbone.

Keep checking the width and the distances forwards and backwards, up and down, with the callipers. When using the callipers, diagonal distances are unreliable, because of the difficulty of maintaining exactly the same angle with the callipers when transferring the measurement. Take all measurements in parallel planes.

The jaw

Apart from the recession of the corners of the eye orbit, probably the most telling feature of the front part of the head is the narrowness of the hoop of the upper jaw, the **maxilla**. If you look up under someone's chin you can see this. It is even more pronounced when the lower jaw or mandible is removed from the main skull, as we saw in Fig 1.5. It is not only narrow but it sticks forward under the nose, creating a bump for the lips to sit on.

The lower jaw seen from below is a V-shape with a flattened point (see Fig 1.6). The teeth, however, match the rounded, narrow hoop of the upper set. This gives rise to hollows, in which muscles sit, between the ascending wings of the mandible and the teeth. Usually the lower front teeth fit up behind the upper set. The teeth need not be detailed unless you are going to model or carve an open mouth.

Muscles

Muscles are either flattish plates or fish-shaped. If you put your fingers on the side of your skull just above your ears and chew, you will feel the plate-like muscle moving. This (the temporal muscle) is fan-shaped, with the point of the fan attached to the front of the **ramus** of the **mandible** (the wing of the lower jaw). Above, it is attached to the rim previously mentioned. The back of the mandible is hinged in grooves in the skull just in front of the ear holes, at the back of the zygomatic arch. The muscle lies fairly flat on the side of the skull, but it effectively fills the space between the zygomatic arch and the cranium. At the same time you can put in the **buccinator** or 'bugler's muscle' which runs from the corner of the mouth through the groove between the lower jaw and the teeth (Fig 2.9). Although I did not do it at this point, at least one of the two pairs of chin muscles used for pulling down the lower lip can be put in at this stage, too.

FIG 2.9 The temporal muscle passes through the zygomatic arch and virtually fills it. The buccinator muscle runs from the outside corner of the mouth inside the ramus of the mandible

*FIG 2.10 Further facial muscles in position: note the orbicular muscle of the mouth, the masseters to either side of the jawbone, the elevators of the upper lip (to each side of the nose). Three different groups of brow muscles can be seen: the large, plate-like **frontalis**, the corrugators of the brow (to either side of the bridge of the nose) and the long **pyramidalis** to either side of the centre line. Once most of the face muscles are done, the eye sockets are ready to receive the eyeballs*

FIG 2.11 The eyeball being placed in the socket shows its size in relation to the rest

Because it has to fit around the arc of the teeth, the muscle surrounding the mouth, the **orbicularis oris**, is longer than it appears. Shape it like a long, thin biscuit. Cut the slot in it before planting it on. The corners should end up behind the bottom of the nose cavity and more or less directly below the middles of the eye sockets.

The next big muscle is the **masseter**, the one which goes from the cheekbone under the outside

corner of the eye to the angle of the lower jaw. The order in which this and the remaining muscles are planted is not important, so long as the inner ones are done first.

On the brow there are various muscles for raising the eyebrows and frowning. You can see in Fig 2.10 how one pair of muscles emphasizes the brow ridge in the middle. Once the brow is done, the eyeballs, about the size of small tomatoes, can be fitted in (Fig 2.11). If you hold a pencil vertically across the middle of your eyeball from the brow to the cheek, it will touch your eyelids or lashes. If you look straight ahead, the pencil held in this position will be seen from the side to slope backwards to the cheek. The front of the eyeball on your model should just touch a pencil held in the same way (see Fig 2.26 on page 38).

The cartilage of the nose is in two parts, but you may give it a nose shape now. Next insert the muscles between the top of the mouth and the cheekbone, and the long one from the inside of the bridge of the nose to the wing of the nostril and the top of the mouth (these are all seen in Fig 2.13). The furrow running from the top of the wing of the nostril to the corner of the mouth is formed by the junction of the two muscles which raise the upper lip, the **levatores labii superioris**, one of which also raises the wing of the nostril. The orbicularis muscle of the eye is formed like that of the mouth and should go on next, although my photographs show a different order. If the texture of the clay is right, as you push it around the eyeball the lids should open (Fig 2.12).

The neck

Now that you have established the position of the chin, you can fasten a spar across the back of the pole to support the neck and shoulders. If it is screwed on there is no risk of disturbing the work already done.

The neck is not a cylinder. The spine, seen from the side, slopes forward as it comes up under the skull. The windpipe and gullet virtually echo the same slope down from under the jaw. The huge **trapezius** muscle slopes down in a curve from the base of the occiput out to the shoulders and then runs down to the middle of the back.

Attached to the mastoid processes are the long, fish-shaped **sterno-cleido-mastoid** muscles that pull down forward and around the windpipe to join the top of the breastbone, the sternum. They both have a head which springs from them down and outwards to the collarbone, giving rise to large hollows in front of the trapezius, which also joins the collarbone (Fig 2.13).

Finishing the modelled head

As you cover the muscles with skin, you will need to pack clay behind and between them. Keep the skin thin; but you must use your judgement in adding the equivalent of fat so that the face looks realistic and healthy.

Begin to make the ears by building out a short tube from the ear hole (Fig 2.14). Then copy the folds from a live model. Notice the **tragus**, the small fleshy projection on the cheek immediately in front of the ear hole or external auditory meatus. Remember that the ears grow out of the gap between the jawbone and the cranium (Fig 2.15).

Do not try to make the head perfectly symmetrical – nobody's is. Nor can one be dogmatic about the shapes, as all heads are different. The important thing is to get plenty of depth in the features so they read well from a distance. When you come to make a head which has soft features, remember that all the bones and muscles are still there; the junctions between them may be very subtle.

FIG 2.12 *The orbicularis muscles of the eyes are in place. The right one has been pushed around the bone and over the eyeball until the eyelids start to open*

FIG 2.13 *The eyes have been completed and the final muscles on the chin and neck planted on. Note the heads of the sterno-cleido-mastoid running onto the sternum and the clavicle. The large muscle from the back of the skull to the shoulder and the outer end of the clavicle is the trapezius*

FIG 2.14 *The whole head is now covered in skin. The ear hole is being developed as a tube; note its position, and the fact that the back of the jaw is no longer a sharp line*

FIG 2.15 *The ear completed and the head finished, apart from the hair*

Carving the head

Three factors make it difficult for beginners to carve a good head. First, we have to reinterpret, in three dimensions, the flat picture we see in our brain, which can make a sculpture look flat and lack depth. Another factor is that in preparing wood for carving, the carver is tempted to cut too closely to outlines (usually working from front and side profiles at right angles to each other), leaving insufficient scope for adjustments as the work progresses. The third factor is that, because we have not studied them, we have mistaken ideas about the shapes of the eyes, mouth and nose and their relationships with the skull. If you have carefully made a clay head, following the method described above, you should be able to avoid the first and the last of these faults.

Typical mistakes in carving a head

Of the two carvings described here, the one in pine (*Pinus sylvestris*) is recognizably a head, but I defy you to find anyone who actually looks like this. In making it I deliberately perpetrated the faults commonly seen in the work of beginners. The head in walnut (*Juglans regia*) more closely resembles reality, and is more deeply modelled. Both pieces are 6¼in (158mm) high (Figs 2.16 and 2.17).

In preparing the wood for the pine head, no thought was given to the proportions of the skull, or to its correct shape in plan view (Fig 2.18). The volume of the hair was also barely considered.

FIG 2.16 Heads in pine and walnut. The pine head, on the left, is designed to show many of the typical beginner's mistakes

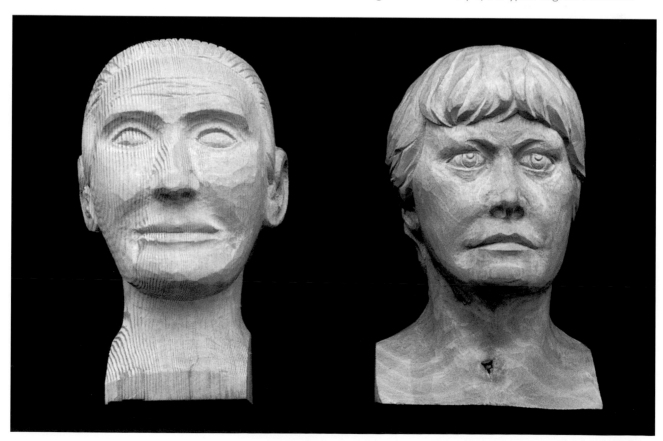

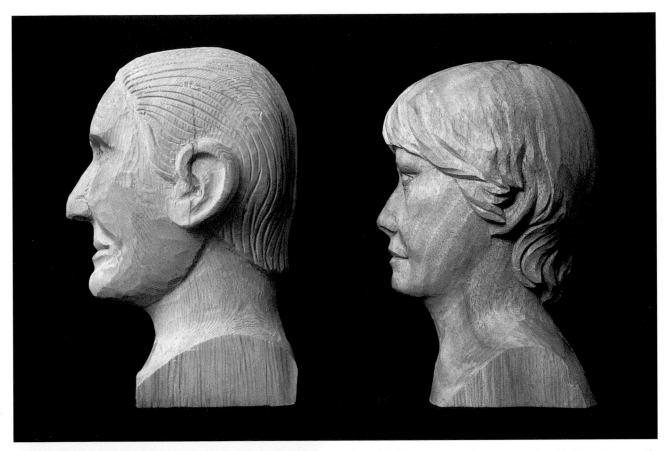

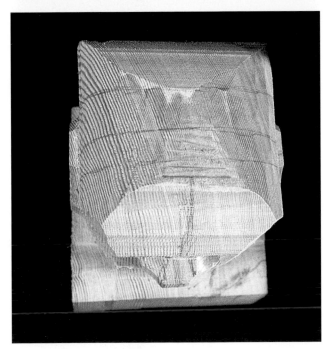

FIG 2.17 *The same two heads from the side. The flatness of the mouth on the pine head and the incorrect placing of the ear are very noticeable. The lines on the forehead and the hair are superficial, with no attempt at three-dimensional modelling*

Proportions

On the human head, the vertical height from chin to crown is approximately the same as the distance from the tip of the nose horizontally to the back of the skull (Fig 2.19). The outside width across the head through the middle of the eyes, including the hair covering the ears, is approximately three-quarters of the total height (Fig 2.20). The line through the middle of the eyes of an adult who still has teeth is halfway between the crown and the chin when viewed from the front. The skull is oval in plan view, with the narrow end at the forehead (see Figs 1.3 and 2.22).

FIG 2.18 *Beginners tend to cut square profiles, with the result that, without a true understanding of the head, the brow can be as wide as the crown*

FIG 2.19 In the unsuccessful pine head, the measurement from the tip of the nose to the back of the hair is less than the height from under the chin to the top of the crown. In roughing out the carving, the bottom of the nose and chin have been determined too soon to allow for any subsequent change in their positions

Beginning the carving

When carving a sculpture, the roughing out is the most important stage. I did several things with the pine head which I have seen inexperienced carvers do. Too many carvers begin by concentrating on the face, without providing for the greater width and height of the skull behind it, so this is what I did (Fig 2.21; see also Fig 2.18). This contributes to the squareness of the head and the loss of proportion. I began straight away by cutting out the side profile of the face, making horizontal saw cuts in under the tips of the nose and the chin. I also established the eyebrows by running a deep gouge across to the bridge of the nose, thus setting

FIG 2.20 (Opposite page) Proportions of a classical Greek head, based on the account in Rhys Carpenter, Greek Sculpture. The head is divided into 10 vertical units and 10 horizontal units, each of which is ¾ of a vertical unit. Greek sculptors usually put something of themselves into their work, so these exact proportions are not often seen

the eyes too deep and making the underside of the eyebrow concave all the way. All these cuts limit one's freedom to adjust the proportions of the head as it progresses.

When preparing the wood for carving, you must make provision for the overall dimensions, including the ears, plenty of hair and part of the neck. In both of the heads shown here, the wood from the chin downwards was kept more or less square so it could be held in a vice. Alternatively it could be held with a bench screw, or screwed to a square block or to the faceplate of a universal vice.

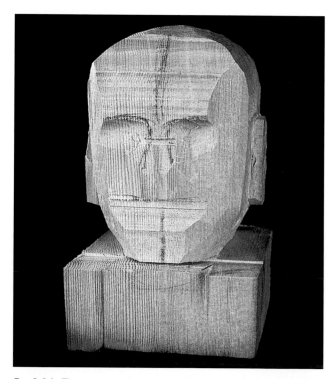

FIG 2.21 The pine head from the front, showing how the eyes have been gouged out before they had a chance, and sharp saw cuts under the nose and chin

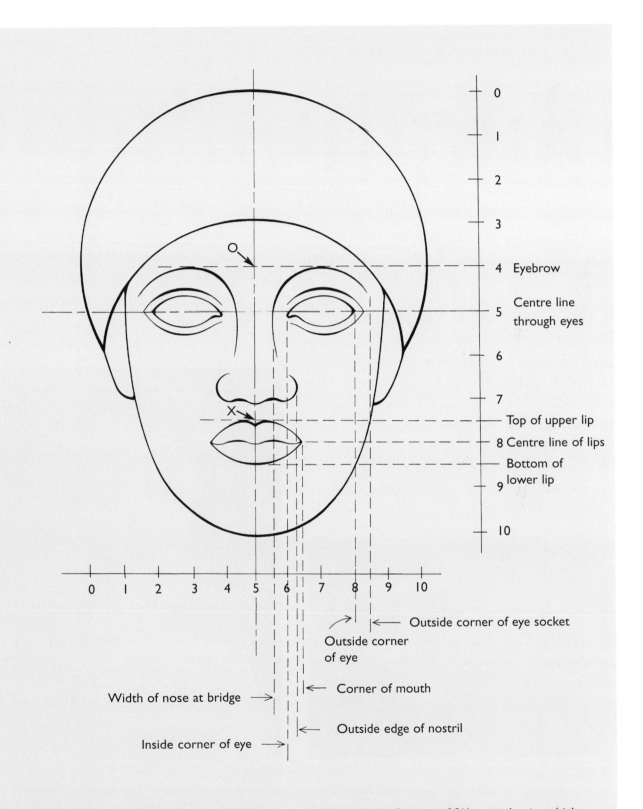

O is the centre of an arc of 4 vertical units which forms the outer line of the hair over the crown and ears

X is the centre of an arc of 2½ vertical units which forms the lower edge of the face around the chin

The importance of the top view

Many people ignore the top view of a sculpture in the round. Yet, even if it is not seen, it is the most important: it dictates the relationships between the side, front and back views, and gives depth to the forms. I began the walnut head by carving the plan view (Fig 2.22). You may prefer to start with the other profiles, but you are less likely to fail if you start this way. The other views were sketched on the wood at the outset merely to ensure they fitted.

It is possible to shape the skull with a broad flat gouge or even a straight-edged chisel, but a deep no. 11 gouge is less likely to tear the wood. It can also be chased easily around the form, cutting across the grain. With a flatter tool you are inclined to work along the grain, which means you are working towards the top view and so cannot see it easily. I always use the largest tool I can, as this speeds up the work; in this case I used a ¾in (19mm) no. 11 gouge.

FIG 2.22 The walnut head is approached in a quite different way, by cutting the top profile first. This means that the front and side views will have to be drawn on a curved surface, but this is not difficult if a centre line is drawn from the chin over the top to the back of the head. The result should be more like a real head

Once the overall top view of the skull has been cut, including the shape of the hair where it is pushed out by the ears, the front and side profiles can be indicated. The rest is left square for holding in the vice.

Front and sides

The front and side profiles of the head of the walnut piece are made without strong undercuts (Fig 2.23). The cut under the side profile of the chin should be made some distance below it; this is because the throat begins far closer to the front of the chin than is commonly realized, and because it is wise to allow for mistakes. Note the

FIG 2.23 The forehead has been cut back to the hairline after shaping the top and back of the head, leaving material where it is needed for the hair and ears. The forms of the face have been given simple planes, with no attempt to fix details at this stage. Pencil marks at the temples indicate the eye line

sloping plane back to the chin from where the tip of the nose is estimated to be: this makes it possible to bring the nose, should you wish, further down the face by paring only a small amount off the tip. This would reduce the distance from the nose to the back of the head, and lead to a corresponding reduction in the height from the crown to the chin.

There is an important principle here which was ignored in the approach to the pine head: if you begin by cutting sharply under the eyebrows, nose and chin, you cannot move these points down the block without eliminating the saw cuts by cutting off the front of the face. In turn, this means losing a large amount of the distance between the nose and the back of the skull, which requires a corresponding shrinkage in height. This may not be too serious if the head is unattached, but if it is on a body it could shrink out of all proportion.

The hair at the front has to be allowed for. Bearing in mind the position of the eyes, carve back to the front of the brow below the hairline from just above the tip of the nose. This gives the approximate slope of the nose. You can also cut around onto the temples. By using a U-shaped gouge, the hairline will not be marked too definitely on the brow. Most of the chisel work so far can be done with ¾in (19mm) or ⅜in (10mm) no. 11 gouges.

Facial features

From the cheekbones down to the jaw line the form can be carved as a wedge, with a blunt edge the width of the nose and chin, down the middle of the face. It helps if the centre line of the head is kept drawn in at all times.

When cutting sharply under the nose of the pine head, I went too far. Many beginners who have never drawn heads fail to notice that the point at which the upper lip joins the **septum** (the partition between the nostrils) is only about halfway back between the tip of the nose and the backs of the nostrils. You can judge which is the correct approach by comparing the two side profiles in Fig 2.17. On the walnut head I merely marked the underside of the tip of the nose with a shallow groove.

Once the temples have been cut, the bridge of the nose can be established. Use a narrow deep gouge, preferably a no. 11, to cut a hollow between the eyeball and the nose (Fig 2.24). The groove can be carved up from the cheek below the middle of the eyeball towards the bridge of the nose and down from the eyebrow to meet it. This should leave a

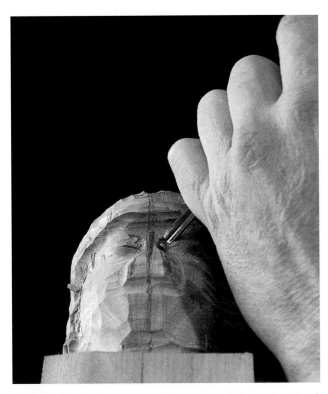

FIG 2.24 *The inside corners of the eyes and the underside of the nose are carved in with a deep gouge*

continuous surface from above the brow across the middle of the eyeball to the cheek. The groove can be carried around below the eye to the temple. Although the zygomatic arch (the thin strip of bone between the bottom of the eye socket and the ear) runs horizontally, make this groove slope upwards onto the temple and around towards the ear as it appears to do in real life.

A no. 5 or even a no. 7 gouge, at least as wide as the eyeball, can be used to cut downwards into the groove below the eye, before or after the cheek has been cut back (Fig 2.25). As mentioned earlier, a simple demonstration of the angle, and of the hollow between the eyebrow and the eyeball, is to get someone to show you their profile while they hold a pencil resting simultaneously on the eyebrow and on the bone of the eye orbit under the middle of the eye. It will usually just touch the eyelids (Fig 2.26).

FIG 2.25 The angle of the eye between the eyebrow and the cheek should be set in early, in this case with an inverted no. 5 gouge

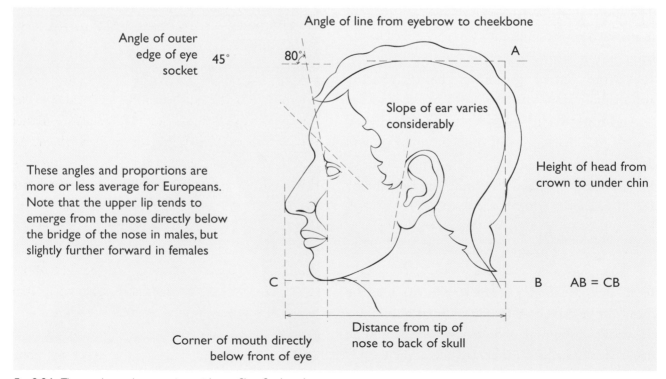

Angle of outer edge of eye socket　45°

Angle of line from eyebrow to cheekbone

80°

A

Slope of ear varies considerably

Height of head from crown to under chin

These angles and proportions are more or less average for Europeans. Note that the upper lip tends to emerge from the nose directly below the bridge of the nose in males, but slightly further forward in females

C

B　AB = CB

Corner of mouth directly below front of eye

Distance from tip of nose to back of skull

FIG 2.26 The angles to be seen in a side profile of a head

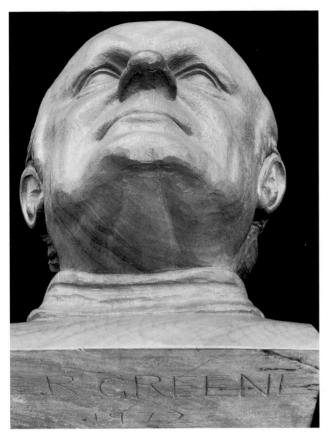

FIG 2.27 The view from below of the head of Edward Greene in African mahogany (Khaya ivorensis) shows clearly how the outside corners of the eyes are further back than the inside corners

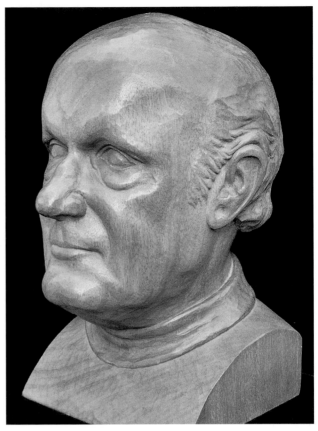

FIG 2.28 A three-quarter view of the same head shows how the effect of the eye on the top of the cheek is exaggerated in an older person. The twist across the eyebrow is also clear

If you look upwards under most people's chins you will see the cheeks slope down and away from the nose. The sharp angle between the nose and cheek occurs only at the wings of the nostrils. To develop the relationship between the eye, the cheek and the nose, make a groove with a no. 11 up from below the cheekbone, running up into the hollow between the eye and the nose. A further groove can be carved from the start of the last cut, up under the zygomatic arch (see Fig 2.32). An examination of the skull will show you that this is following the upward slope of the lower edge of the cheekbone. This makes the cheekbone prominent and should help in pushing the cheek around the corner, thereby giving depth to the face.

Now you can make a sloping cut up from below the middle of the eyeball, around the eye socket into the outside corner of the eye, and another downwards to form the step of the bone that is the outer edge of the eye socket. Seen from the side, this is often about 45° above the horizontal (see Fig 2.26). Look up underneath the chin of your carving and deliberately push the outside corners of the eyes further back than the inside corners (Fig 2.27). The eyeballs push out the flesh above the cheek, so take up far more space than that enclosed by the eyelids (Fig 2.28).

Now is the time to establish the tip of the nose. Do not cut in straight, but go across underneath it with a deep gouge. Noses may be more or less sharp, but the tip is always rounded in both front and side profiles and when seen from above. From below it often resembles a strawberry with its slight dips above the wings of the nostrils. In profile the underside of the nose in the middle usually curves around onto the upper lip, although some people have a sharp angle here. As carving the insides of the nostrils involves undercutting, it should be left until the rest of the face is finished.

Since the teeth form a large bump under the nose (Fig 2.29), slope the mouth back and around the side of the face to a point vertically below the front of the eyeball, when the face is upright. If you look up from under someone's chin you will see that the slope back from the middle of the upper lip towards the back of the jaw is steep and gently curved, with a slight step behind the corner of the mouth.

FIG 2.29 The mouth is always kept forward at the middle, under the nose, but extra wood is left for the lips. The middle of each eye is still in a continuous line from the brow to the cheek; only towards the inside and outside corners is there any hollow under the brow

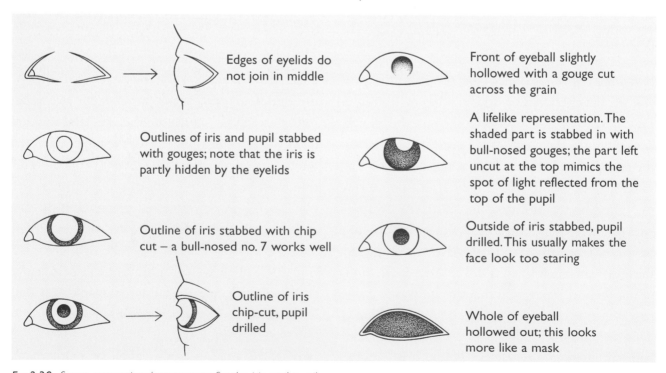

Edges of eyelids do not join in middle

Outlines of iris and pupil stabbed with gouges; note that the iris is partly hidden by the eyelids

Outline of iris stabbed with chip cut – a bull-nosed no. 7 works well

Outline of iris chip-cut, pupil drilled

Front of eyeball slightly hollowed with a gouge cut across the grain

A lifelike representation. The shaded part is stabbed in with bull-nosed gouges; the part left uncut at the top mimics the spot of light reflected from the top of the pupil

Outside of iris stabbed, pupil drilled. This usually makes the face look too staring

Whole of eyeball hollowed out; this looks more like a mask

FIG 2.30 Some conventional treatments for the iris and pupil

Eyelids

Another beginner's mistake is to carve the eyelids before the eyeballs have been shaped. When you are ready, mark in the eyelids with a single cut using a ⅛in (3mm) no. 11. This makes the head look asleep (see Fig 2.31). Later the eye can be opened by stabbing the edge of the lid down to the eyeball with a no. 5 gouge. Do not aim horizontally, but cut on a radius towards the centre of the sphere.

I have avoided making the eyelids look like spectacles, partly by letting the brow droop to cover most of the upper lid. In reality, the rounded edges of the eyelids and the eyelashes soften the outlines of the eyes. They are not sharp. The dead look can be avoided by one of the conventional treatments of the pupil shown in Fig 2.30. Note that the whole of the iris is not normally visible. It is possible to achieve a lifelike effect without cutting the eyelids all the way around, leaving them flush with the eyeball just above and below the middle of the eye.

The mouth

The mouth should be carved at the same time as the outside of the nostrils and the chin. On the walnut head the nose is a trifle long, with the result that the mouth is rather low on the face. A common mistake is to carve the groove between the lips before the overall shape of the outside of the mouth has been established. When this has been done, note that in side profile this groove is wider and deeper than you may have thought. If you look at the side profile you will also see that I have kept the middle of the upper lip up to its junction with the septum, or partition between

the nostrils, further forward than the bridge of the nose; this is more common on women than on men. The red parts of the lips form a useful marker, but their edges are often only a matter of colour. If necessary they can be indicated by a slight change of plane or a small groove.

The corners of the mouth cause many problems. Usually when someone's mouth is closed and at rest, the lower lip is slightly overhung at the corners by the upper lip. On both lips the surfaces of the ordinary face skin and the red part twist. On the lower lip the face skin at the corner of the mouth slopes inwards and upwards (Fig 2.31). However, under the middle of the lower lip it faces downwards (Fig 2.32). The red part faces forwards in the middle and upwards at the corners. Likewise in the middle of the upper lip, where the **philtrum** (the groove running down from the septum) meets the dip in the upper lip, the surface of the ordinary skin tends to face upwards and the red part of the lip faces forwards. As the chisel follows the red of the lip towards the corner it ends up facing downwards. The skin above twists until it faces forwards; this often gives rise to a slight hollow running diagonally across the top of the lip at the corner. The ridge left above it may fade into and merge with the ridge running down from above the nostril, or it may disappear into the groove below that ridge (Fig 2.33).

Hair

After the face, the hair can be tackled. Even on apparently straight hair, unless it is plastered down, there are individual locks which move rather more than the furrows on the pine head suggest. These furrows are both too symmetrical and, like the lines on its forehead, just grooves cut

FIG 2.31 *The chisel is held so that the blade can indicate the inward slope of the outside of the lower lip at the corner. The eyelids have been started by a simple gouge cut, so that the edge of the lid is not cut hard down to the eyeball in one go; this allows for subsequent correction of its position*

FIG 2.32 *Pencil lines indicate the hollows running from below the cheekbone to the inside corner of the eye and under the cheekbone back to the zygomatic arch in front of the ear. Other lines indicate other hollows including that running across the corner of the upper lip. The sweep of the cheek onto the side of the nose above the wing of the nostril is also shown*

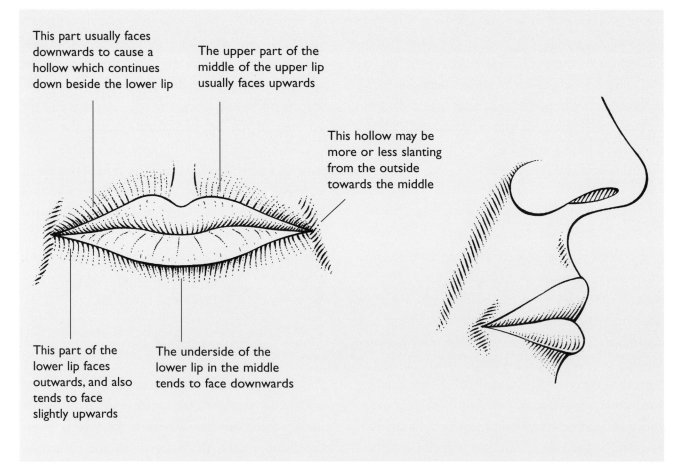

This part usually faces downwards to cause a hollow which continues down beside the lower lip

The upper part of the middle of the upper lip usually faces upwards

This hollow may be more or less slanting from the outside towards the middle

This part of the lower lip faces outwards, and also tends to face slightly upwards

The underside of the lower lip in the middle tends to face downwards

FIG 2.33 *The complex relief of the mouth and surrounding areas can only be grasped by careful observation of living models, but here are some features to be aware of*

into a surface. Real locks have volume and shape, and are separated from one another by pronounced grooves (Fig 2.34). They need to be planned when doing the roughing out.

The hair on the walnut head was mostly shaped with a V-chisel, tilted in places to give movement and depth. Some of the grooves were deepened by chip cuts with a no. 4 fishtail gouge (Swiss no. 3F). Detail is mainly confined to the ends of the hair, although in some styles carvers have covered the whole surface with tight curls or intricate waves, using V-tools and shallow gouges with rounded ends. The ears are mostly hidden, but the bottom lobes can be seen growing out of the back of the jaw.

Ears

The ears are not as difficult as many think. At first glance they seem wildly crumpled, and vary considerably not only from individual to individual but also from one side of the head to the other. However, they do normally have the same elements. The most important thing is to site them correctly. They will be at different heights at each side of the head, but the top will usually be near the level of the eyebrow (Fig 2.35), and the bottom level with the middle of the upper lip. They start just behind the back of the jawbone. From the front their join with the cheek is invisible. The main feature is the **helix**, which

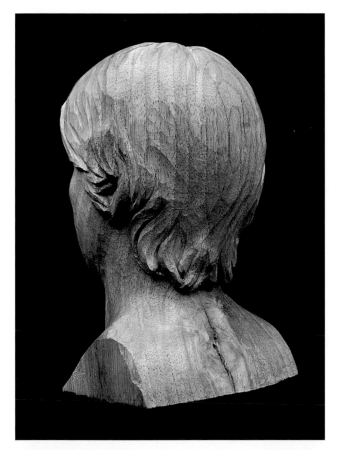

FIG 2.34 *The back of the walnut head, showing that plenty of wood was left for the hair; note how it is picked up by the backward slope of the neck. Most of the detail is kept to the ends of the locks*

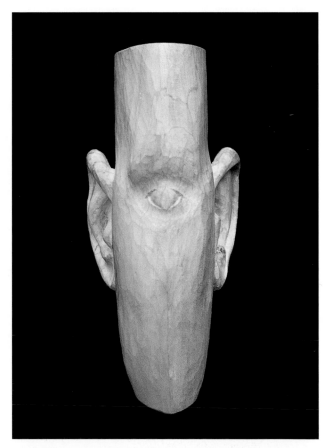

FIG 2.35 *A sculpture by Dick Onians in spalted maple (Acer campestre) to demonstrate the shapes of ears. The positioning of the ears on the head is close to nature. In this view, the beginning of the ears is hidden behind the cheeks*

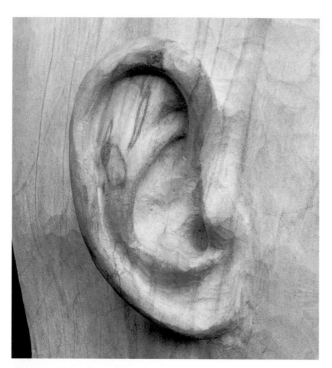

FIG 2.36 The right ear from the side, showing the interlocking spirals of the helix and antihelix, with the furrow in the latter, and the lump of the tragus overhanging the actual ear hole

looks like a C with the bottom end tailing off into the lobe at the bottom. In front of the ear is the tragus, a triangular projection growing out of the back of the cheek (Fig 2.36). The ear hole lies just behind the tragus, but the hollow around it is bordered at the lower edge by the **antitragus**. This forms the upper boundary of the lobe, and usually has a small bump on it. The antitragus curves round, roughly parallel with the helix, to become the **antihelix**. Seen from in front, this sometimes projects further than the helix behind it (Fig 2.37). The helix spirals down into the hollow behind the tragus, while the antihelix curves up behind the spiral to produce the effect of two interlocking Cs. There is a groove in the antihelix at its top end. You can simplify the shapes to make

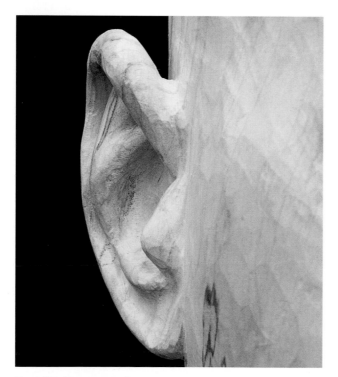

FIG 2.37 Front view of the ear, showing the projection of the tragus and the anti-helix. In this case the antihelix does not stick out further than the helix, which can be seen behind it

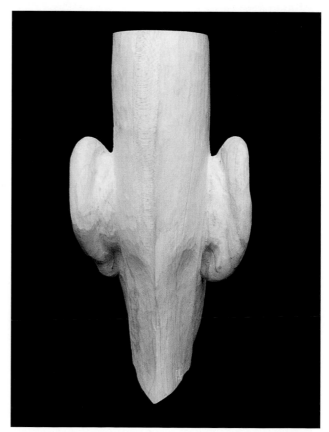

*FIG 2.38 Back view of the ear sculpture, showing how far the ears project from the head; note the tubular shape of the **auricular cartilage** as it joins the ear to the head*

them look less crumpled, and you may be surprised by how beautiful ears can be. Notice how much they project from the head (Fig 2.38).

Incidentally, the piece of wood that was used for this sculpture, being spalted, was brash and crumbled when carved across the grain even with the sharpest chisels. The problem was solved by painting the wood with paraffin (kerosene) (Fig 2.39). The amount of colour which this leaves in the wood is negligible. Liquid paraffin, which is sold as a laxative, also works, but does not penetrate so far, as it is viscous. This also means that it takes a month or two to evaporate. Its advantage is that it does not smell.

While carving, the two key things to bear in mind are that the bone structure dictates the final shape, and that the top view is the most important view. If you carve a portrait, you will find that once you

FIG 2.39 *The top of the ear, facing the left side of the picture, is end grain. The sample on the lower right, carved across the end grain, illustrates the problem of crumbling which was cured by applying paraffin. The slight pink dye in the paraffin is not noticeable on the wood*

have the bones right the head will look like your subject even without details of eyelids and lips (Fig 2.40). If you look at heads from all angles, but especially from above and below, you will make something that is truly three-dimensional and not a series of four flat profiles.

FIG 2.40 *The bone structure of Edward Greene is sufficient to make his head recognizable, although details are not yet carved*

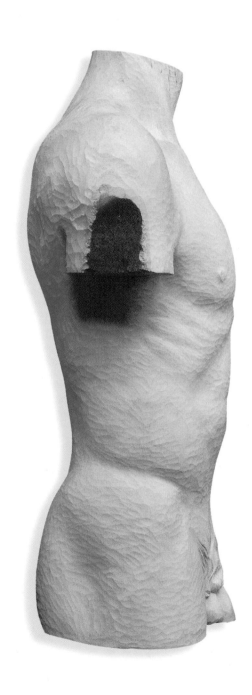

Chapter

THE TORSO

The idea of sculpting the human torso without head and limbs would probably not have occurred to man if he had not been attracted by the wreckage of ancient civilizations such as those of Greece and Rome. Because the torso is the most solid and compact part of the body, many torsos have survived where the rest of the figure has broken and been lost. Today it is sculpted both as a form in its own right and as a component of a complete figure. In this chapter it is used as an exercise, in the same way as the head in Chapter 2 and the legs, feet and hand and arm are treated in the following chapters. It would appear the same if the rest of the figure were added.

Seventh-century BC Greek figures look like those modern wood sculptures where front and side profiles have been cut out with a bandsaw and the corners rounded. But in 300 years the Greeks shook off the stiffness of their first attempts and learned to produce lifelike figures. Their aim was a god-like perfection, and mathematical proportions were seen as divine (see Fig 2.20). The result was that, as each carver tried to make his sculptures more alive than his master's, he also made the forms as close to the ideal as possible. It is, in any case, easier to plan a sculpture if there are

set proportions for the parts of the body. Those employed by the Greeks differ from those of the Middle Ages; in parts of the East today, other centuries-old systems are still followed. Ancient Greek sculpture developed because its makers did not observe their canons rigidly.

With the Greek example in mind, carvers wishing to represent the human form should try to improve upon, rather than copy, existing sculptures. By drawing and modelling, and by anatomical study, you will quickly learn how the various lumps and hollows are formed, which parts can change shape, and which are hard and soft. Though fat, **fascia tissue** (such as the **carpal tunnel** which holds in the tendons travelling through the wrist) and skin soften the details of bones and muscles, they cannot hide them altogether; nor can clothes.

Learning the bones and muscles

As with the head, carvers of the human figure will find invaluable a good knowledge of the underlying structure and the main muscles visible at the surface. They should then be able to avoid making square, disjointed and impossibly contorted figures. A good way to start is by modelling the torso in clay. The armature is uncomplicated and there are no arms to get in the way of the ribcage and its muscles.

As before, remember that true modelling involves building up from the inside, not carving excess clay from a block. When modelling a torso you do not usually work from so far in as is shown here, but it is worth doing once to learn why the surface is as it is.

The backbone

We start with the spinal column, spine or backbone, which separates the shoulders from the pelvis. It is made up of 33 or 34 vertebrae (24 excluding the sacrum and coccyx; see below), with **intervertebral discs** between those above the pelvis. The bumps which you can feel down the middle of your back are long processes which grow backwards from every vertebra. They are sometimes known as 'spines', which can be confusing. The erect spinal column seen from front or back is a straight line, but seen sideways it is gently S-shaped (Fig 3.1; see also Figs 1.1 and 1.2). At its base in the small of the back, or lumbar region, it curves backwards; five vertebrae are here fused together to form the sacrum, which continues the same curve, tapering into the coccyx, comprising a further three, four or even five fused vertebrae, which curves forwards again. Above the lumbar region the spine curves backwards as it ascends, and then forwards from near the top of the ribcage or thorax. It returns more or less to the vertical at the top of the neck, where it fits under the middle of the skull. Seen from behind, the sacrum is roughly triangular and links the two halves of the pelvis.

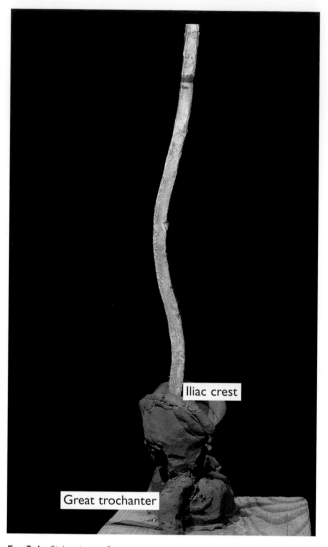

FIG 3.1 *Side view of an armature on which a torso is being built up with clay. The front of the body is to the right. The aluminium wire has been rammed into a hole in a piece of softwood and bent to the shape of the spinal column. The iliac crest and the great trochanter (the outside of the head of the femur) are clearly seen*

The pelvis

The pelvis forms a half-cup shape to hold the intestines and other organs (Figs 3.2 and 3.3). But the parts that interest the sculptor most are:

- the outer rim, or iliac crest, that runs from the sacrum up, around and down at the front to

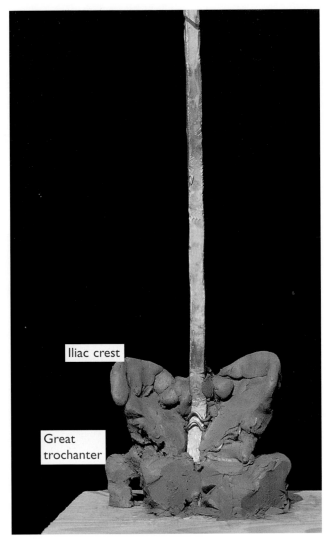

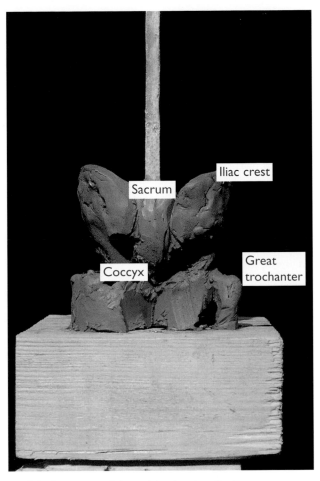

FIG 3.3 Rear view of the pelvis, showing the iliac crest swinging down to meet the sacrum at the lower end of the backbone, and the coccyx; labels indicate the sacrum (above) and the coccyx

*FIG 3.2 Front view of the armature showing the cup of the pelvis and the top of the femur set into the **acetabulum**, its socket in the pelvis. The iliac crest at the top of the pelvis is also shown*

the anterior superior spine (the bony lump just in from the side of the body below the waist) at each side;

• the **symphysis pubis**, the part which we do not see because it is behind the genitals, but to which are fastened some of the **adductor** muscles that we use to pull the legs together;

• the hip socket (**acetabulum**), in which the top of the thighbone (the femur) sits. The acetabulum is also invisible, because the ball on

the head of the femur is on the end of a short stalk almost at right angles to the main shaft of the bone. On the outer side of the bone at the top is a large, rounded projection, the great trochanter. The hip is normally widest across the trochanters, although this may not be the case on a plump person.

Lumps (or processes), ridges, spines and plates of bone are where strong muscles are attached. The pelvis is composed of large plates with thick rims and, being in the middle of the body, has numerous powerful muscles attached.

The ribcage

The gap between the highest part of the iliac crest and the lowest rib is at least a finger's thickness, generally more. It is possible to build the ribcage or thorax rib by rib, but it is safe to regard it as basically egg-shaped, with the little end at the top, and the bottom end cut off (see Fig 1.9). The ribs curve in towards the spine and appear to form a valley down the back, with the row of vertebral spines standing out in the middle (see Fig 1.8). In a well-muscled back these spines barely project, unless the back is bent forwards. The two bottom ribs at each side are unattached at the front; they are said to be 'floating'. The ribs above them are linked at the front by cartilage, which arches up to the **solar plexus** at the bottom end of the sternum. The sternum is a jointed bone that runs from this point to the top of the thorax. From the front it appears dagger-shaped, but viewed sideways it curves and slopes backwards to the neck. The top five ribs are joined to it by more or less horizontal strips of cartilage, which flattens out the middle area of the thorax.

On the model shown, the thorax is made out of expanded polystyrene, which is light, easily shaped and, when anchored with wire to the spinal column, stops the clay from sliding down (Fig 3.4). Wire can be pushed through it to support the tops of the arms.

The shoulder girdle

The arms are easily moved in many directions, because they are joined to the thorax only by muscles and have only a small bearing surface where the collarbones (clavicles) rest at each side of the top of the sternum.

FIG 3.4 *Right-hand side of the polystyrene core of the thorax, showing how the sternum slopes back towards the neck*

The shoulder blades (scapulae) are attached to the back by muscles; they are roughly triangular plates, curved to fit the thorax (Figs 3.5 and 3.6). Near the top, which is the short side of the scapula, there is a ridge or 'spine' that slopes across to the outside corner and projects beyond, forming the acromion process on which the clavicle rests (Fig 3.7). At the front there is a similar projection, the coracoid process. The head of the upper arm bone, the humerus, sits in a socket on the corner of the scapula below and between these two (Fig 3.8). You should be able to feel the clavicle and the processes when the arm hangs naturally. You can also feel the great tuberosity which sticks out on the side of the humerus opposite the joint, a little lower than the acromion process.

Spine of scapula

FIG 3.5 Back view showing the scapulae planted on

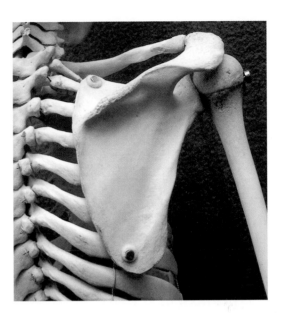

FIG 3.6 Back view of the shoulder joint on an actual skeleton

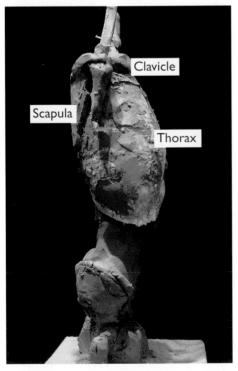

Clavicle

Scapula

Thorax

FIG 3.7 Side view of the armature showing the clavicle, scapula and thorax. The acromion process at the top front of the scapula is seen passing across the top of the humerus to meet the outer end of the clavicle

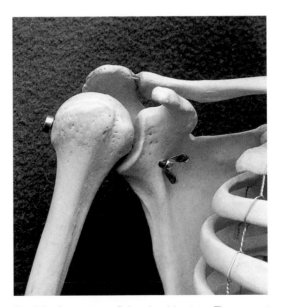

FIG 3.8 Front view of the shoulder joint. The acromion process is visible above the head of the humerus, with the clavicle just touching it and the coracoid process swinging forward under the clavicle

If you look at the skeleton from above (see Fig 1.10) you can see how the curvature of the thorax makes the edge of the scapula nearest the spinal column project. The result is that the surface slopes forwards from there to the arm when the shoulders are relaxed. The clavicles seen from above curve around the top of the thorax, then swing forward to the front of the acromion processes.

From the front the clavicles often present a virtually straight line, unless the arms are raised. On the model the left arm is raised to show how the clavicle and the scapula move and the muscles change when the arm stretches upwards. The same plan is followed in the carved example below.

Putting on the muscles

There are interior muscles and organs that affect the surface form, but these are of much less importance to the sculptor than the superficial muscles (Fig 3.9). Muscles contract, harden and change shape when they are used. By adopting various postures and pushing and pulling, you can feel what most of them do.

The muscles of the back and side

Let us start at the bottom with the **gluteus maximus** (no. 10 in Fig 3.10), the big muscle that we sit upon. It is the body's strongest muscle, used in making the body erect and in bending the thighs. It attaches to the back of the iliac crest, and emphasizes the triangular area at the top of the cleft of the buttocks, formed by the junction of the sacrum with the pelvis. It slopes diagonally forwards and outwards from the back of the iliac crest, joining the rear part of the **iliotibial band** behind the great trochanter. Seen from the side

FIG 3.9 *Side view of the finished clay model, showing how the fibres of the muscles are marked*

(Fig 3.11 no. 15), this band of fascia tissue is Y-shaped. It runs tapering down the outside of the thigh and is attached to the top of the shinbone at the knee. The great trochanter sits in the angle of the Y. The front arm of the Y is joined to the **tensor fasciae latae** (19), which continues up to the anterior superior spine of the pelvis.

The **gluteus medius** (9) is a fan-shaped muscle which springs from the iliac crest between the gluteus maximus and the tensor fasciae latae, with its point on the great trochanter. Because there is usually some fat on the hips and buttocks, the grooves between these three muscles are softened,

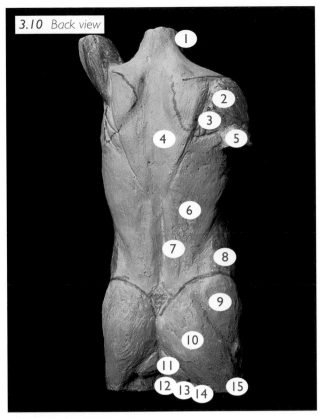

3.10 Back view

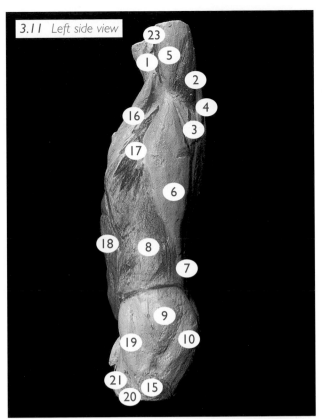

3.11 Left side view

The clay model was cast in plaster and the muscles coloured for ease of identification. The blue lines indicate scapulae, iliac crest, sacrum, clavicles, sternum, and the lower edge of the ribcage at the front

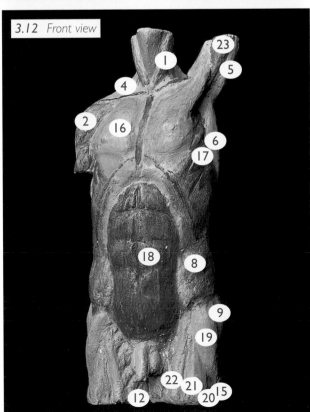

3.12 Front view

Key to the muscles

1	Sterno-cleido-mastoid	12	Adductors and gracilis
2	Deltoid	13	Semitendinosus
3	Teres major, teres minor and infraspinatus	14	Biceps femoris
		15	Iliotibial band
4	Trapezius	16	Pectoral
5	Triceps	17	Serratus magnus
6	Latissimus dorsi	18	Rectus abdominis
7	Aponeurosis of the latissimus dorsi	19	Tensor fasciae latae
		20	Vastus externus or vastus lateralis
8	External oblique	21	Rectus femoris
9	Gluteus medius	22	Sartorius
10	Gluteus maximus	23	Biceps of the arm
11	(Fat)		

but the great trochanter either stands out or sits in a hollow, depending on fat and posture. Also attached to the anterior superior spine of the pelvis is a long, thin muscle, the **sartorius** (22), which, seen from the front, runs diagonally across the front of the thigh to the inside of the knee. Between the sartorius and the tensor fasciae latae is the **rectus femoris** (21). The sartorius creates a groove between this and the group of adductor muscles, which form the inside of the thigh.

The main visible muscles of the back are the **latissimus dorsi** (6) and the trapezius (4). The latissimus dorsi (literally 'the widest of the back'), is attached by a large, flattened tendon or **aponeurosis** to the lower half of the spine, including the sacrum, and the back of the iliac crest. It swings upwards and outwards, crossing the bottom corner of the scapula and twisting up into the armpit to attach to the front of the top of the humerus. You can feel and see it when you raise your arm. From behind, it makes the back seem to taper inwards from the armpits to the waist.

The two trapezius muscles together resemble a huge kite with its bottom point in the middle of the back, overlapping the two latissimus dorsi muscles. It forms a V-shape up to the inner ends of the spines of the scapulae, runs along the tops of these spines to the meeting with the clavicles, then up to the base of the skull and down to the clavicles at the front. It is the muscle that makes the shoulders slope up to the neck and makes the base of the neck wider at the back. Muscles that run under these alongside the backbone also affect the outer shape.

Attached to the underside of the outer third of the clavicle, to the acromion and to the underside of the spine of the scapula, is the **deltoid** (2). This attachment is like the baseline of a triangle, the apex of which is almost halfway down the humerus. Slotting up under the deltoid at the back is the **triceps** muscle (5) which runs down the back of the upper arm.

The muscles seen from the front

The muscles of the side and front (Fig 3.12) consist mainly of the breast (**pectoral**) muscles (16), the **external oblique** muscles (8) and the **rectus abdominis** (18). The pectoral muscle is a large, plate-like muscle which is attached to the inner part of the clavicle, the sternum and the cartilage below. Its head twists to a point which is inserted under the deltoid onto the humerus. If you push your fingers up between it and the latissimus dorsi, you can feel the ribcage sloping up towards the base of the neck. The nipple sits on this muscle near its lower outer edge; on a woman the mammary glands sit on top of this muscle.

Emerging from under the front edge of the latissimus dorsi and sloping downwards to the front of the thorax is a row of finger-like heads, which belong to a muscle called the **serratus magnus** or **serratus anterior** (17). They form a zigzag groove where they slot into the external oblique (8), a tall muscle that is attached at the bottom to the iliac crest and at the top to the lower eight ribs. It particularly swells out above the iliac crest. It is joined to its pair by a large flattened tendon or aponeurosis which completely covers the rectus abdominis from top to bottom. At its bottom edge it joins **Poupart's ligament** which runs from the anterior superior iliac spine to the symphysis pubis, immediately behind the genitals. This ligament forms the curved furrow, the inguinal furrow or fold, between the abdomen and the thigh – a feature which has often been exaggerated in sculpture, particularly by the ancient Greeks. The rectus abdominis (18) is an oblong muscle running from the arch at the bottom of the thorax down to Poupart's ligament. When well developed, it presents a great column with a groove down the middle to the waist, crossed by three horizontal grooves (also exaggerated in Greek art, and in much Renaissance and later work), the lowest of which passes just above the navel.

At the top of the sternum, the windpipe runs up in front of the spine, surrounded by the thyroid and the thyroid cartilage. From the side, this makes the front of the neck slope up and forwards, echoing the slope at the back. However, at the front the two sterno-cleido-mastoid muscles (1) come down from the mastoid processes on the skull just behind the ears to form a V with its point at the top of the sternum. These muscles are particularly noticeable in women and in men with thin necks when they turn their heads. From each of them another head swings out near the bottom to join the clavicle. This means that, when seen from the front, while the trapezius is tapering out to the shoulders, the front of the neck tapers in the opposite way.

The differences between male and female bodies are dealt with in Chapter 7, carving the whole figure (see also Figs 1.17–1.19).

The difference between a cast taken from life and a sculpture

One of the most pathetic objects I have seen, yet one of the most instructive, was a plaster cast of the torso of a girl who had drowned in the Seine during the 1890s. There must have been a time when all art schools had a copy. What struck me most was the flatness of the forms. From a distance they could not be read, but all merged together without defining shadows. The living form has varying colours and movement, even if it is only the pulse under the skin, the almost imperceptible rise and fall of the ribcage in breathing, or a flicker of the eyes. These supply that missing depth which can only be shown in sculpture by some sort of exaggeration.

When Rodin submitted his *Age of Bronze* sculpture of a male nude to the Paris Salon, it looked so lifelike that he was accused of taking a mould from a real person. Eventually the jurors were convinced he had not, as, like all good sculptors, he had omitted some details and exaggerated essential forms to create the shadows needed to make the figure readable. In modern art schools this skill is seldom taught, and because the emphasis is now on ideas and not on execution, it is fashionable to take casts from live models. I find this sad, as the rigorous demands of looking, understanding and interpreting are avoided, and the figure produced is more bland and eerie than impressive. Besides, from a distance it seldom reads well.

Beginners' errors

Having built up a torso as described above, you should avoid the pitfalls encountered by many beginners when you come to carve one.

At first glance the body appears cylindrical, with cylindrical arms, legs and neck, but if you make a body like this, even if you pay attention to grooves and bumps and put them in, it will look wrong. The first will be a symbolic body, the second a symbolic body with surface decoration. If, after roughing out your carving, you realize the underside of the buttocks should be lower than the crutch, or the armpit should be well below the top of the shoulder, it may be too late.

If, however, you know the shapes of the pelvis, the spine and the hip joint, you will get the right relationship between the crutch and the buttocks. If you remember that the thorax is like a slightly flattened egg with the little end at the top, and how the clavicles and scapulae fit on it, the waist and shoulders will be recognizable. If you know that the scapula has a spine that runs across the back to the outside of the shoulder, you will not, as some carvers do, make a groove that follows the inside of the arm right up to the top of the shoulder, effectively separating the arm from the body as on a doll.

The composition of the torso shown on the following pages draws attention to the changes in the shapes of the muscles according to how they are used. The carving of the female body in Chapter 7 demonstrates how putting the weight onto one leg makes the pelvis tilt and the buttocks change shape. It also shows how the different distribution of fat on the female body, the wider pelvis and less pronounced musculature, make the outer shape differ from a man's.

Carving the torso

My purpose in carving this torso is to show how to carve down to the essential bones and muscles, and how to develop the forms to give the sculptural depth which an exact copy from life

would lack. A carver must recognize that the material he uses is different from that of the human body, and consequently he inevitably puts something of himself and his material into the work. Not even the most cunning replica maker can reproduce every pore, hair and variation of the surface. Like Rodin, you have to compensate for their absence by simplification and exaggeration, even when making a representational carving. Having accepted that you are using a different material from the original, and acknowledged that you are incapable of copying it absolutely, you should resign yourself to being an artist and give the world something of your own unique understanding and vision. Nevertheless, you should treat your first carvings of the human figure as exercises in getting to know the structures, so that later you can take informed liberties with them.

It takes so long to carve a torso that you cannot expect a model to pose for you while you do it. It is therefore essential to attend a life class to learn the shapes of the body. The above modelling exercise will help, then quick reference to your own body while you work should fill any gaps. If your own physique does not appeal to you, you could imitate the ancient Greeks and idealize the human form, as I have done with this carving which is based on my own torso.

I used green sycamore (*Acer pseudoplatanus*) for this carving. There was a slight spread at one end of the log which seemed suitable for the raised arm, so I could get a torso almost two-thirds life size. To make it as big as possible, I left some bark on the outside of the hanging shoulder and lost a little width on the hips. This is acceptable, as some men are narrow there.

Scaling down

I used a simple way of scaling down to any proportion (Fig 3.13). For this method you need a pair of callipers that can measure the largest dimension on your body. You also need a board and a large sheet of paper (or a stretch of wall), and a long straightedge.

Draw a baseline at least as long as the maximum dimension on your body and, with one point of the callipers resting on one end of the line, describe an arc from the base line upwards. From intersection of this arc with the baseline, and with the callipers set at the maximum length obtainable from the wood (compatible with the width and depth dimensions), draw another arc to cross the first. With the straightedge you now join these intersections and the end of the baseline to create a triangle. It is easy thereafter to mark off on the baseline and the diagonal the distances measured on your body. If you then connect these points, you will find you get a series of parallel lines indicating the corresponding dimensions on the carving. By noting what measurements these lines record, you can quickly check your carving as you work in towards the finished form. Don't try to measure every last detail – it is incredibly boring and will make for a lifeless carving.

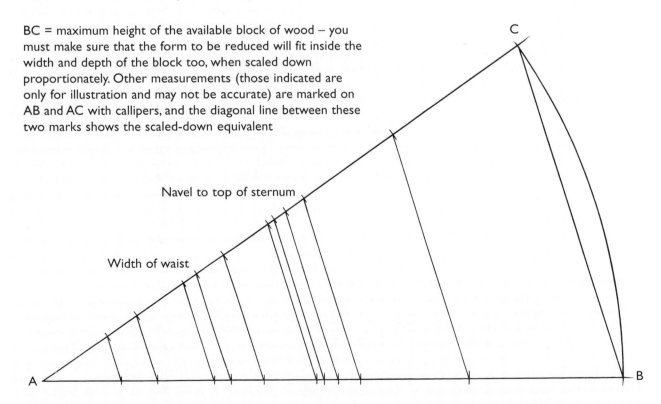

AB = AC = distance from top of neck to just below crutch

BC = maximum height of the available block of wood – you must make sure that the form to be reduced will fit inside the width and depth of the block too, when scaled down proportionately. Other measurements (those indicated are only for illustration and may not be accurate) are marked on AB and AC with callipers, and the diagonal line between these two marks shows the scaled-down equivalent

Navel to top of sternum

Width of waist

FIG 3.13 A method for scaling down. The baseline represents the length of the actual object. The long diagonal is the same length. The short, parallel diagonals give the equivalent measurements on the block of wood

FIG 3.14 *Front view of the wood chainsawn to rough shape. The bottom of the ribcage is indicated. The gap between the neck and the raised arm is not yet cut through*

FIG 3.15 *Back view of chainsawn block. The shoulder blades are already visible*

FIG 3.16 *Side view of chainsawn block with the original clay model, showing the outline of the pelvis drawn on the wood to establish the position of the great trochanter*

Useful measurements

Helpful distances to record are those between the anterior superior iliac spines, between them and the crutch, between crutch and navel, navel and bottom of sternum, and the length of the sternum. Useful, too, are the width and depth of the thorax at particular points, the width outside the heads of the great trochanters, the interval between the dents where the posterior iliac spines meet the sacrum (see Fig 3.19), and the width between the backbone and the outer ends of the scapulae. All these points should be marked on the wood, and redrawn as they are cut away.

You may not realize, until you measure it, how much the shape of the neck varies from the top of the sternum to underneath the chin. You will probably have other surprises. In my case I was surprised to find the dimensions of the raised shoulder somewhat larger than the neck below the chin.

The positions of the nipples are also useful, as are the lower edges of the pectoral muscles at the front, the latissimus dorsi and trapezius muscles on the back, and the gluteus maximus and medius and the tensor fasciae latae on the buttocks and hips.

Roughing out the carving

When roughing out the sculpture, leave about $1/2$in (13mm) waste all around. In some places it will be more. If one arm is raised, it is best at first to keep the interval between the neck and the body as small as possible, to allow for changes of plan and possible accidents. Indeed, it is wise to

FIG 3.17 *Side view showing the forms further developed with a deep gouge, used across the grain*

FIG 3.18 *The auger was used to drill several holes up from below to speed the drying. Major features marked on the wood are the outline of the thorax, the right clavicle, Poupart's ligament running down from the anterior superior iliac spines, the navel, and a vertical centre line through the sternum*

make it a rule in all carving not to carve spaces between forms until the outside shapes – in this case, the right side of the neck and the outside of the left shoulder – are at least clearly established, if not finished.

I used a chainsaw to create profiles quickly, defining the neck, the raised arm, the cut-off hanging arm and the slopes of the spine forward to the neck and in to the small of the back (Figs 3.14–3.16). It also marked the hollow formed by muscles on each side of the spine. (Although this might be thought of as an inside shape which ought to be left until outside shapes are defined, it

is safe enough since it marks the central line.) I used an Arbortech industrial disc on an angle grinder to further shape the waist, hips and shoulders, but because the wood was green it was easy to carve by hand. **Remember that both chainsaws and angle grinders are dangerous tools, and must never be used without the proper safety precautions and protective clothing. Attendance on a recognized chainsaw training course is strongly recommended.** Further roughing out was done with a ¾in (19mm) gouge (Fig 3.17), and it would have been quite possible to use hand tools alone.

Once the positions of major forms had been established, I used a hand auger (Fig 3.18) to drill holes as far up inside as I dared, both to allow the

FIG 3.19 *Back view showing the spine of the right scapula marked, and the V which indicates the flattened area caused by the sacrum. The crosses at the top of the V are where the iliac crest joins the sacrum; there are often dimples in these places*

FIG 3.20 *The front, showing the gradual working in of the forms. The gap between the neck and the raised arm is still blocked at this stage. Note how lines are carved away as carving progresses; it is not always necessary to reinstate them later*

FIG 3.21 *The back view, showing the effect of deeper muscles beside the spine in the small of the back as they push out the aponeurosis or flattened tendinous area at the bottom end of the latissimus dorsi*

FIG 3.22 *Side view at the same stage. The grooves around the gluteus medius are visible on the hip, and the lower front edge of the thorax is defined*

wood to dry from the inside and to reduce weight. Although the carving was really too heavy for the universal vice which I used, it was possible to move the piece around more freely than if held any other way. Without it, I should have had to screw a block onto the base so I could hold it in a vice or with clamps.

Most of the detailed carving can be done with a ½in (13mm) no. 11 gouge – or a no. 9 or no. 10

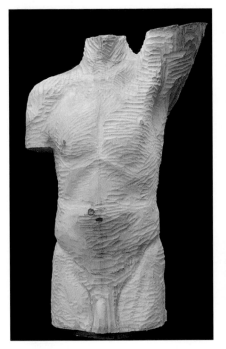

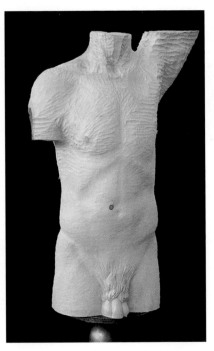

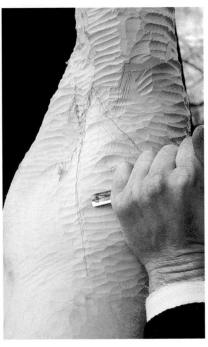

FIG 3.23 The lower abdomen and the tops of the legs are about to be finished. Note further development of the external oblique and pectoral muscles. Positions of the nipples are marked, and the left armpit begins to appear. Only now is the neck separated from the raised arm

FIG 3.24 The lower part of the torso and the genital region have been finished with shallow gouges

FIG 3.25 Using a bull-nosed no. 7 gouge to work close to the final shape of the latissimus dorsi where it passes over the bottom end of the scapula and moves into the armpit. Note that as the arm is raised the scapula swings around the back towards the side

will do as well. This is used principally to carve across the grain, working around the forms, but some forms may be outlined with grooves first to fix where the lowest parts should be (Figs 3.19–3.24). Deep hollows demand a no. 8 or 9 spoon-bit gouge of about the same width.

Finishing

The surface is refined with a bull-nosed no. 7 gouge (Fig 3.25) and finally with a bull-nosed ½in (13mm) no. 3. Their rounded ends make it easier to use these gouges in hollows, as the corners are less likely to catch in the wood. Occasionally it will be necessary to use a flattish spoon-bit in deep

hollows, and in one or two places I used a 1¼in (30mm) Swiss no. 2 gouge, flute-down, to create a smoother effect.

On a piece of this size a very smooth finish is not needed – indeed, I find the worked surface more exciting (Figs 3.26–3.28). Not only does it have a softer look, like skin, it also holds the light and shade and emphasizes the modelling of the form rather than bouncing light off and drawing attention only to the surface.

The wood was finally protected with a coat of Danish oil, as linseed oil would have made it too yellow, and wax would have been caught in any roughnesses.

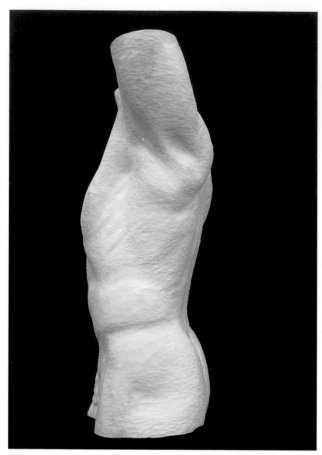

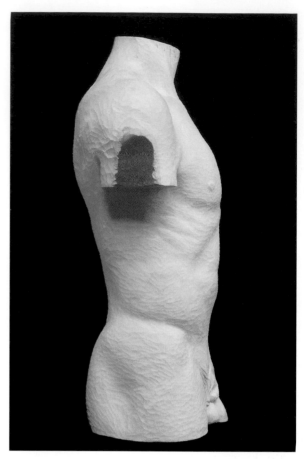

FIG 3.26 *The left side of the finished torso, showing the shape of the armpit when the arm is raised. See Fig 3.11 for identification of muscles*

FIG 3.27 *The right side. The black mark on the shoulder is a patch of bark. Notice how the front edge of the ribcage slopes back and down to the waist*

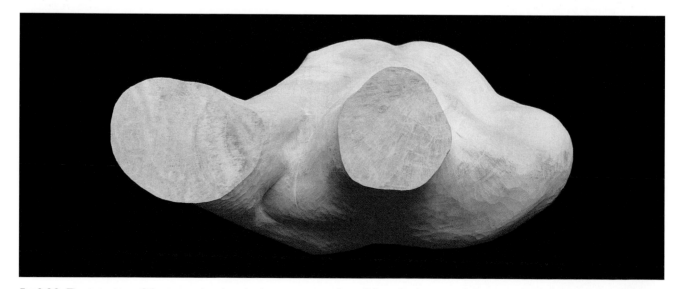

FIG 3.28 *The top view of the torso, showing the large cross section of the raised arm and the curve back from the front of the thorax to the shoulders. The slope of the spine of the right scapula to the shoulder is clear. Note the cross section of the neck*

The patterns that emerge during carving

You will find that consciously or, more likely, unconsciously, you are developing patterns out of the anatomy. For instance, if you look at the photograph of the back of the finished torso (Fig 3.29) you will see the diamond formed by the **sacrospinalis** muscles. These are the ones that run under the aponeurosis of the latissimus dorsi muscle beside the backbone from the sacrum to between the scapulae. Notice, too, the way the inward slope of the buttocks is in line with the upper sides of this diamond. At the front (Fig 3.30) there is a correspondence between the lower edge of the relaxed pectoral muscle and the external oblique, and between the bottom edge of the thorax and the hollows of the groin. In subsequent sculptures one might choose to develop these patterns further. In ancient Greek figures, in particular, patterns such as these are often exaggerated.

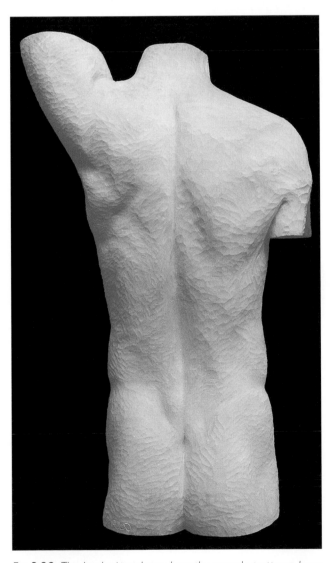

FIG 3.29 *The back view shows how the muscle patterns have been slightly exaggerated*

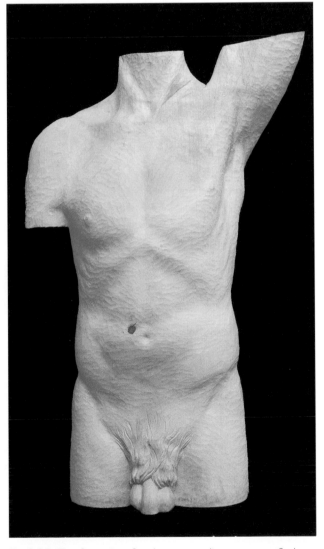

FIG 3.30 *The front view. See how many lines you can find that echo or mirror each other*

THE KNEES

Quite apart from the importance of the limbs as parts of the body, there is in them a rich source of sculptural shapes. They repay close attention. Knees fascinate us – think of knobbly knees competitions – yet, as with other parts of the human anatomy, how many of us really know their shapes? This chapter concentrates on the knees, but relates them to the rest of the leg.

If the leg is shown straight, the knee may be acknowledged by a carver as a slight bump at the front, and at the sides and back as a narrower place than the thigh or calf. When the leg is bent, it is often treated like a bent or curved cylinder, or the knee is made sharp. In fact, legs are composed of complex shapes that change according to activity. They are certainly not regular like tubes, nor sharply angular.

The bones of the leg

In dealing with the torso we have already seen how the leg joins the body, and the beginnings of some of the muscles. Here we concentrate on the leg just above and below the knee. The lower leg and the foot are dealt with in the next chapter.

The knee is a hinge in the middle of the leg. It is the meeting place of three long bones, and the joint is protected in front by the kneecap or patella (Figs 4.1 and 4.2). It is operated by a number of powerful muscles above and below, which are most easily seen in the leg of an athlete (Figs 4.3–4.5).

FIG 4.1 *The patella in front of the right knee. Above the patella is the femur (thighbone); below, the tibia (shinbone) and the much smaller fibula*

Although only small parts of the bone structure in the knee joint and the front of the shinbone (tibia) are visible on the surface, they are present in the overall shape of the leg, and their rigidity and directions must never be forgotten when carving. Above the knee the thighbone (femur), the longest bone in the body, slopes inwards from the hip joint to the knee. The wider the pelvis, the greater the

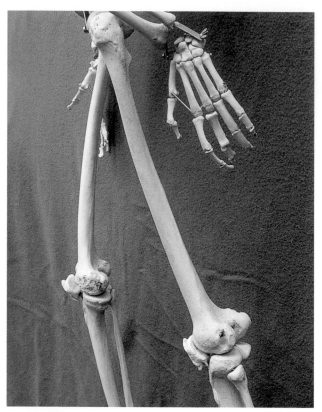

FIG 4.2 *Side view of the outside of the left knee and inside of the right knee*

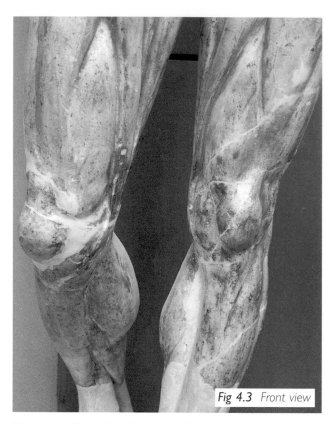

Fig 4.3 *Front view*

The knees of the 'flayed' man; the flayed man gives a good idea of the volumes of the muscles

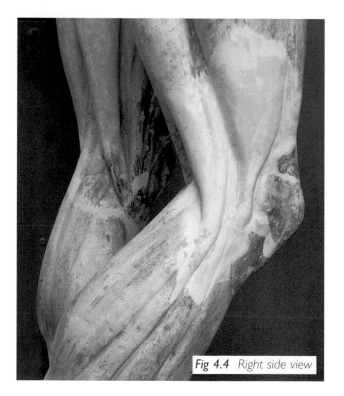

Fig 4.4 *Right side view*

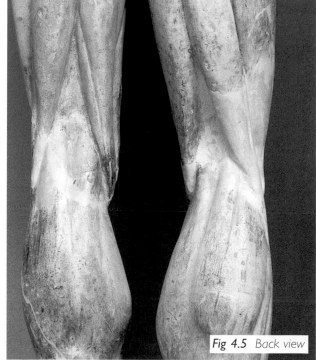

Fig 4.5 *Back view*

degree of slope (a woman's pelvis tends to be wider than a man's; compare Figs 1.1 and 1.2). This slope is most obvious on the outside of the leg when looked at from in front or from behind. On the inside of the thigh, bunches of muscles, particularly the adductors – the ones we use for pulling our legs together – make the outline more or less vertical at the top. The femur, in the side view, hangs vertically from the pelvis but has a slight backward curve (see Fig 4.2) which emphasizes the fullness of the curve on the front of the thigh, and puts the knee of someone standing upright behind the furthest forward part of the thigh. At the knee end the femur has two large projections (the inner and outer **condyles**) at the sides, which have powerful muscles attached to them.

Since the joint with the bones of the lower leg is a hinge, the leg can bend in only one plane. It is further limited in that from the straight it can bend only backwards. Covering it in front, the kneecap is a flattish, almost triangular bone pointing downwards.

The two bones of the lower leg are the tibia (Latin for 'trumpet') and fibula ('brooch'), which is a thin rod (Fig 4.6). The tibia or shinbone can easily be felt, as it presents a sharp edge to the front that appears to slope from the knee inwards to the ankle, where its head is the inner malleolus or inner anklebone. The fibula in most positions is invisible at the surface except as the outer malleolus, although its top end does project if the leg is bent and the foot turned inwards.

The muscles and tendons

Many powerful muscles meet at the knee, connecting it above to the pelvis and below to the

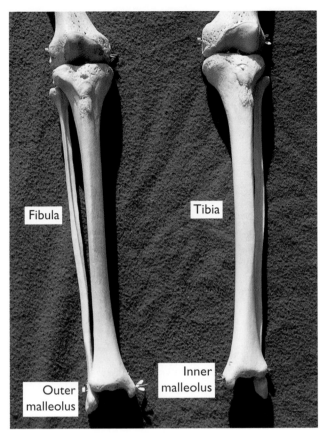

FIG 4.6 *The bones of the lower leg from the front, with the patella removed to show the joint surfaces*

foot. Under the fleshy covering, most are shaped rather like long fish. They taper at the ends, usually into long, hard tendons, which can sometimes be easily seen. The **Achilles tendon** at the back of the ankle is the most obvious. You can also often see a big one running from the back of the outer malleolus up into the side of the calf, and can see, or at least feel, three others at the back of the knee (Figs 4.7–4.10).

Whether there is much fat present or not, all these elements affect the shapes on the surface. Even if they do not have sharp grooves between them or form definite ridges, they do create planes and quicken or flatten curves. Lights shone at different angles across the leg can pick up shadows that indicate hollows.

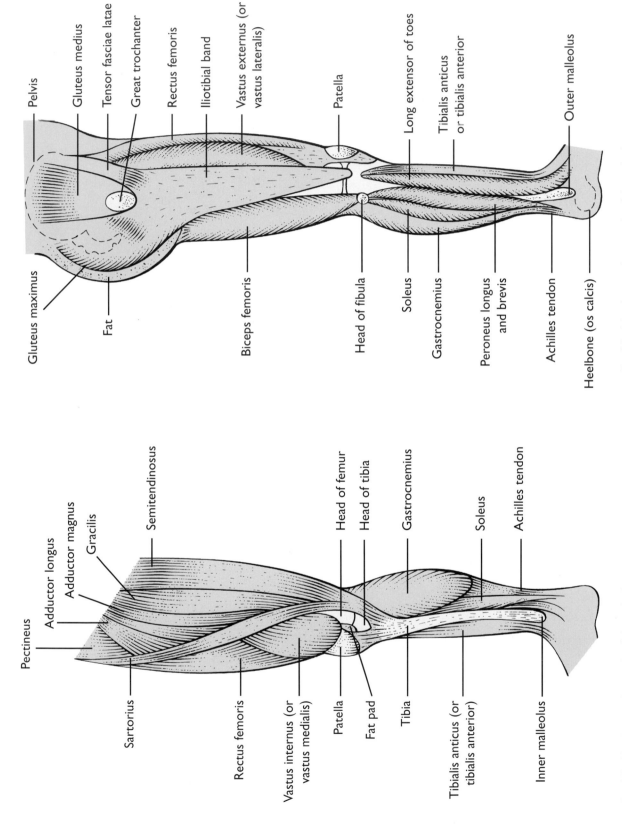

Pelvis

Gluteus medius

Tensor fasciae latae

Great trochanter

Rectus femoris

Iliotibial band

Vastus externus (or vastus lateralis)

Patella

Long extensor of toes

Tibialis anticus or tibialis anterior

Outer malleolus

Gluteus maximus

Fat

Biceps femoris

Head of fibula

Soleus

Gastrocnemius

Peroneus longus and brevis

Achilles tendon

Heelbone (os calcis)

FIG 4.8 *Muscles on the outside of the right leg*

Pectineus

Adductor longus

Adductor magnus

Gracilis

Semitendinosus

Head of femur

Head of tibia

Gastrocnemius

Soleus

Achilles tendon

Sartorius

Rectus femoris

Vastus internus (or vastus medialis)

Patella

Fat pad

Tibia

Tibialis anticus (or tibialis anterior)

Inner malleolus

FIG 4.7 *Muscles on the inside of the right leg*

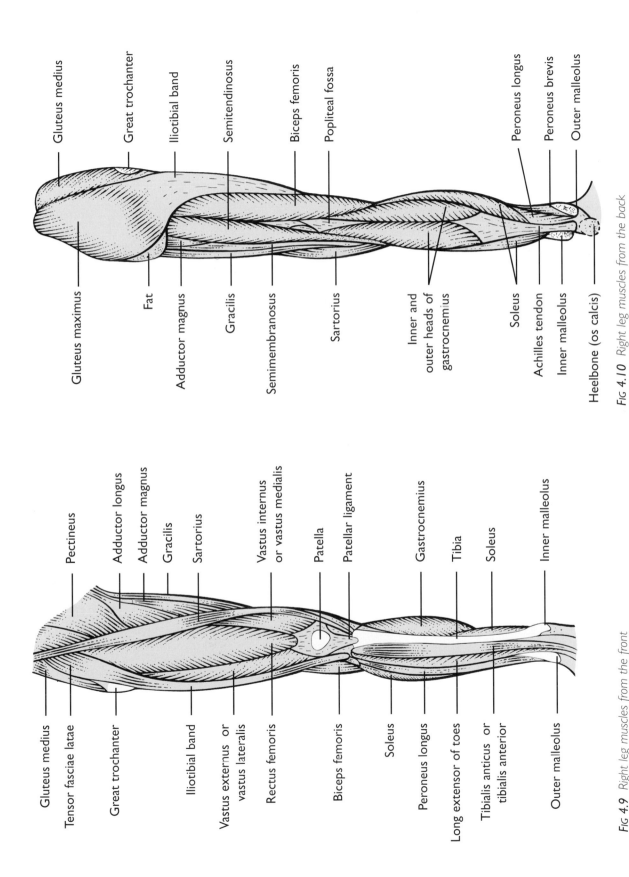

Gluteus medius

Great trochanter

Iliotibial band

Semitendinosus

Biceps femoris

Popliteal fossa

Peroneus longus

Peroneus brevis

Outer malleolus

Gluteus maximus

Fat

Adductor magnus

Gracilis

Semimembranosus

Sartorius

Inner and outer heads of gastrocnemius

Soleus

Achilles tendon

Inner malleolus

Heelbone (os calcis)

Fig 4.10 Right leg muscles from the back

Pectineus

Adductor longus

Adductor magnus

Gracilis

Sartorius

Vastus internus or vastus medialis

Patella

Patellar ligament

Gastrocnemius

Tibia

Soleus

Inner malleolus

Gluteus medius

Tensor fasciae latae

Great trochanter

Iliotibial band

Vastus externus or vastus lateralis

Rectus femoris

Biceps femoris

Soleus

Peroneus longus

Long extensor of toes

Tibialis anticus or tibialis anterior

Outer malleolus

Fig 4.9 Right leg muscles from the front

Carving the knees

To illustrate the carving of knees I decided to show one straight and one bent, as in the act of climbing a step (Fig 4.11). This meant that they had to be connected by sufficient wood to keep them related as they are in life, and to provide strength and stability to the finished piece.

FIG 4.11 *The finished carving of the knees*

Part of the joy of knees is in the shapes of the leg around them. However, in order to keep the knees connected and at the same time visible all around, it was necessary to include wood above and below them that could have been carved to make the adjoining parts. Since carving these would have distracted from the knees and from the overall composition, these parts have been left in the block. Where possible, I left the outside of the log intact. By tackling the project in this way it was possible to make a unique object, which incidentally could serve as a stool. The following description shows a method of tackling such a problem, and draws attention to the main features of the legs and some of the ways in which their shapes can change.

It is unlikely that you will find a model who is not only available when your drawings fail to supply the information that you need, but also is of the right size to be copied directly into your wood. My available model was myself. The largest available log was from a plane tree (*Platanus* sp.). Being from a branch, it contained reaction wood: the cross section was oval, with the pith near the underside of the branch. After lying untreated for three years, the log had developed large end shakes. It had already been cut into reasonable lengths, so these shakes had not progressed too far. Rather than risk their spreading further and ruining the log, I decided to carve it unseasoned. However, this meant I had to be prepared for abnormal movement and splitting – though in the event, interestingly, no shakes or warping occurred. One advantage was that, being green, the wood was comparatively easy to carve. Because this log was not big enough, I had to reduce the size of the carving to about four-fifths of life size, using the method of scaling down described in Chapter 3 – although this slowed the carving process, because measurements could not be taken direct from the model.

Learning the shapes before carving

It is important that you at least make drawings, and possibly a clay model, before you begin (Fig 4.12). Even so, you will probably find some information lacking when it comes to the carving. Profile drawings of front, back and sides are not enough: you should try to indicate qualities of cross-sectional curvature. It does not matter how messy your drawings are. Even if you cannot read your own drawings, you will have forced yourself to look and see things you may never have noticed before. Having this knowledge will allow you to carve faster and more fluently.

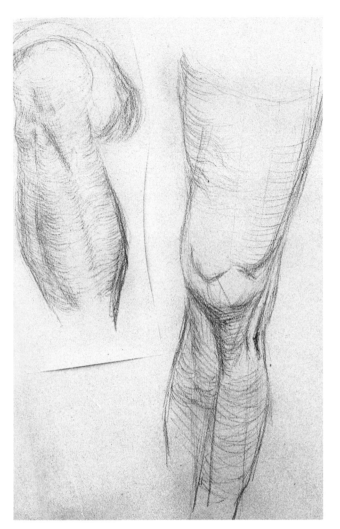

FIG 4.12 *Initial studies in charcoal on sugar paper*

FIG 4.13 *Front view of the finished composition, showing the vastus externus (or vastus lateralis) on the outside of the left leg, the knee below it, and below that the top of the lower leg sloping outwards and parallel with the inside of the knee. You can see the inward slope of the right thigh and the virtual ridge formed by the rectus femoris at the top. The small bump on the outside of the knee is the head of the fibula*

In this composition the straight leg is cut off about a quarter of the way down from the knee. The muscles of the lower leg are much the same shape as those of the bent leg, although all muscles change shape when the leg is used differently. For instance, to make the knee more obvious in the straight leg I have tensed the thigh muscles as in standing on tiptoe. The right leg, which is bent, has the muscles of the thigh disposed as if it were about to climb a stair. If it were seated, the pressure of the seat would distort the muscles on the underside; as it is, they hang relaxed. The tendons on the back of the bent knee are more obvious on each side (see Figs 4.11 and 4.19). Note, too, that the patella on the bent knee moves towards the outside (Fig 4.13).

FIG 4.14 The composition roughed out with chainsaw and angle grinder

I began the carving as usual with general shaping, using a chainsaw and an angle grinder with a wood-cutting disc. It is, however, quite possible to rough out the work using hand tools. When working on a rough log like this, measurements are necessarily imprecise, so allow plenty of extra wood. Once crude profiles have been cut, the surfaces are near enough square for closer profiles to be drawn on them (Fig 4.14).

Profiles and planes

Your study of legs should have taught you the main features of the profiles. Seen from in front, the straight leg may not be vertical. However, unless the feet are apart, the inside of the thigh descends from the groin vertically to about halfway to the knee. At this point the thigh is pushed in by the sartorius (tailor's) muscle, which

FIG 4.15 *The profiles of the left leg and right calf are beginning to emerge. Gouge work starts to create inward slopes at the tops of the thighs where the sartorius presses them in*

runs down from the forward edge of the iliac crest of the pelvis diagonally across the front of the thigh and tucks in under the inside surface of the knee. On the outside, the muscles follow the inward slope of the bone from the great trochanter at the top of the femur to the side of the knee (see Fig 4.13) . The two shapes together emphasize the inward movement of the knee.

On the outside of the knee, the tendon of the **biceps** of the femur runs parallel with the inside of the knee, which appears to fall vertically. Below the knee, the profiles of the **gastrocnemius** and **soleus** muscles, the large muscles on the back of the calf, make the leg appear to change direction yet again and echo the inward slope of the thigh (Fig 4.15; see also Fig 4.13).

Seen from the side, the back of the straight leg tapers in from under the buttock towards the knee (Fig 4.16). This is because the bulk of the muscle is in

FIG 4.16 *The backwards thrust of the left leg is started. The sag of the muscles under the right thigh is noticeable, and the tendon of the biceps femoris is shown running from them to the back of the knee. The carving is still considerably oversize at this stage*

FIG 4.18 *From the back, the tendon of the biceps femoris runs vertically along the outside of the left knee. Above it the iliotibial band swells out. The gastrocnemius disappears up into the popliteal fossa between the biceps femoris and the combined tendons of the sartorius, gracilis, semimembranosus and semitendinosus muscles. The bulge of the gastrocnemius is visible on the right calf*

FIG 4.17 *Back view of the right leg showing the division between the two heads of the gastrocnemius, and the Achilles tendon tapering down from them with the soleus muscle visible on each side of it. Note how the muscles of the thigh slope from the outside to the inside*

the upper part of the thigh. The lower part of the muscle consists largely of the tendons that join onto the bottom end of the femur and the tops of the tibia and fibula on each side. This theoretically leaves a hollow called the **popliteal fossa**, but in practice this is bridged with muscle (see Fig 4.10). Running into this fossa from the lower leg are the two heads of the gastrocnemius muscle, which in side view presents a long, flattish slope down and backwards. This drops in to join the Achilles tendon about halfway to the heel (Figs 4.17 and 4.18).

The side profile of the front of the thigh shows it curving slightly forward from the top, then turning backwards down to the knee (Figs 4.19 and 4.20). The knee is somewhat behind the furthest forward part of the thigh. The kneecap is a bump, usually with a hollow above it. You can feel it and move it from side to side and up and down; some people can even get their fingers behind theirs. The profile below it looks like a continuation of it, but is actually formed partly by the tubercle or knob on the top front of the tibia and partly by the patellar ligament. To complicate matters further, there is a fat pad behind the ligament. The tubercle flows into the anterior (front) crest of the tibia, which is the sharp ridge of bone you can feel. Its profile is

FIG 4.19 The finished left knee from the side, showing the groove under the vastus externus above the patella, and the tendon of the biceps femoris coming down to the side of the knee

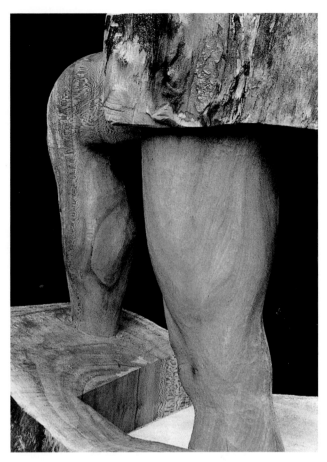

FIG 4.20 Here the gastrocnemius can be seen running into the popliteal fossa, and just beyond it the bump formed by the tendons of the sartorius, gracilis, semimembranosus and semitendinosus muscles as they join the head of the tibia

disguised by the **tibialis anticus** (or **tibialis anterior**) muscle which runs from the head of the fibula down to the ankle, but the bone reappears again lower down, where you can feel it as it swings inwards and forwards to the ankle joint, forming the inner malleolus (Fig 4.21). From the side of both straight and bent legs, the back of the gastrocnemius appears more or less parallel with the underside of the kneecap and patellar ligament.

The front and side profiles of any part of the body are only silhouettes; they do not tell you of the changes in shape when you look from other angles. It is not easy to see the way shapes change

if you look along the leg, although standing on a mirror or looking up or along the leg of a life model does help. For instance, the sloping plane on the top of the thigh is easily seen when the leg is bent (see Fig 4.13). Planes are a useful guide and should be carved early in the roughing out.

You can detect planes by placing straight, rigid strips, such as wooden or steel rulers, across them and looking down on them. If you do this you will see, for example, that each side of the gastrocnemius is flattened and slopes forward. Likewise you can see, when the knee is bent, that the inner tendons on the underside of the thigh –

FIG 4.21 The right knee defined with a Surform rasp. The patella is clearly seen, with the tubercle of the tibia below it and the tibialis anticus or tibialis anterior muscle (marked in pencil) beginning to swell over the front of the tibia. On top of the thigh, the swellings of the vastus externus muscle and the more prominent vastus internus are visible

FIG 4.22 The right knee from the side, showing the hollow between the iliotibial band and the biceps femoris, the way the muscles hang down lower on the inside of the thigh, and the effect of the tendons on the thigh immediately behind the knee. The head of the fibula is just visible, as is the downward slope of the gastrocnemius onto the soleus below it

those of the sartorius, gracilis and semitendinosus muscles where they attach to the side of the tibia – are lower than the tendon of the biceps femoris on the outside (Fig 4.22).

Another test is to wrap a piece of soft wire or a thin strip of lead around the leg, taking care not to press it into the surface. If it goes only part of the way around, it can be pulled off to give a clear indication of cross sections, particularly if the points where it

was in contact with the surface are marked on the leg with chalk or pencil. If you are carving a leg full size, the wire can be used as a template.

The bent leg

The bent leg shows how shapes change when the leg is in a different position. In this case the leg is not actually in stress, merely resting. The result is that the muscles of the thigh hang down and, on the outside, slope under and inwards more than they do on the straight leg, where the back is more rounded. The patella moves towards the outside of the knee but otherwise stays in virtually the same position, with the result that, as seen from the front, the outer condyle of the femur, which is masked by the patella in the straight leg, now stands out slightly above it (Fig 4.23; see also Figs 4.21 and 4.22). The inner condyle of the femur also changes its position and its appearance. You should be able to see these changes on a life model and feel them on yourself. The information in this book cannot replace your eyes or your sense of touch; the more you draw and model the shapes, the easier it is for you to remember them while carving.

Depth

As with all carving of animals or humans, it is important to give greater rather than less depth to forms, and to avoid squareness. Where there are grooves between muscles or other parts of the surface form, do not keep them constant – they seldom are, but merge or vary in depth. They may be isolated with a deep gouge or V-tool just to indicate their position and direction when bosting (roughing) out, but even on the most well-muscled man they do not appear as separate islands on the surface.

Fig 4.24 shows the hand tools which were used most in carving this study.

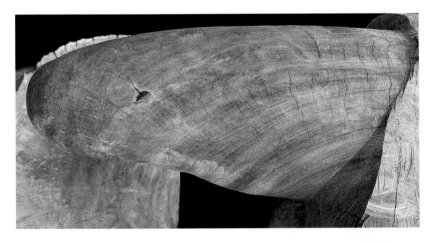

FIG 4.23 The right thigh from above, showing how the taper towards the knee differs on the inside and outside

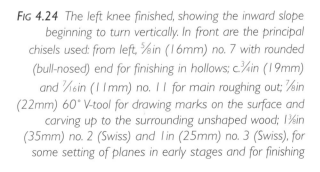

FIG 4.24 The left knee finished, showing the inward slope beginning to turn vertically. In front are the principal chisels used: from left, ⅝in (16mm) no. 7 with rounded (bull-nosed) end for finishing in hollows; c.¾in (19mm) and ⁷⁄₁₆in (11mm) no. 11 for main roughing out; ⅞in (22mm) 60° V-tool for drawing marks on the surface and carving up to the surrounding unshaped wood; 1⅜in (35mm) no. 2 (Swiss) and 1in (25mm) no. 3 (Swiss), for some setting of planes in early stages and for finishing

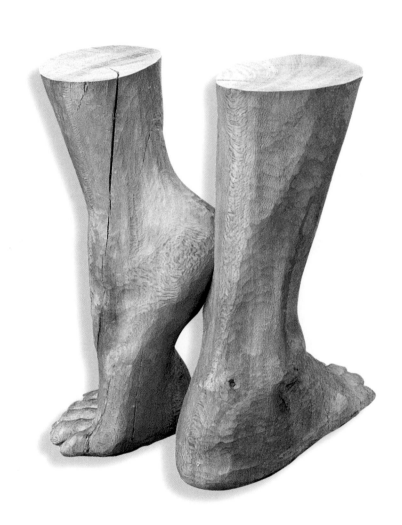

THE FEET

It cannot be often that a writer deliberately embarks on an utterly pedestrian subject. Many students doing life drawing omit the extremities of hands, feet and head. This is partly understandable, as hands and heads you can see on clothed people all about you, and you might be expected to have some idea of their shapes. Feet, however, are usually encased in footwear. To omit them from a drawing of a standing model is also to miss the important point that all the weight of the standing body is concentrated on them. Not all feet are equally beautiful, but they are all full of interest, particularly if the anklebones are included. As we seldom make feet on their own, as I have done here, their relationship with the leg should also be learnt, so in this study I have included part of the shins and calves. This also made a satisfying composition (Fig 5.1).

Carving the feet life-size concentrates the attention on both the underlying structure and the superficial details, and is more revealing than reducing their scale. One foot alone is enough to teach the essential shapes, but by doing two together it is possible to show how they can change in different positions, and to make a more interesting sculpture.

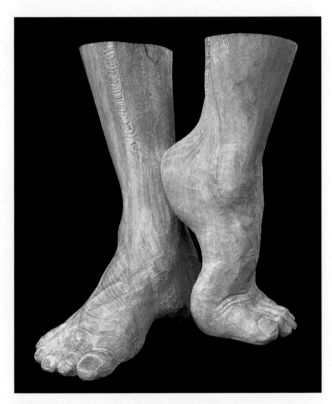

FIG 5.1 *Finished study of feet in plane wood*

Learning the shapes

As with carving any part of the anatomy, the ideal is to have a model you can first study by drawing, and subsequently refer to while carving. Many carvers may choose to do as I have done here and be their own models, but at least some drawings

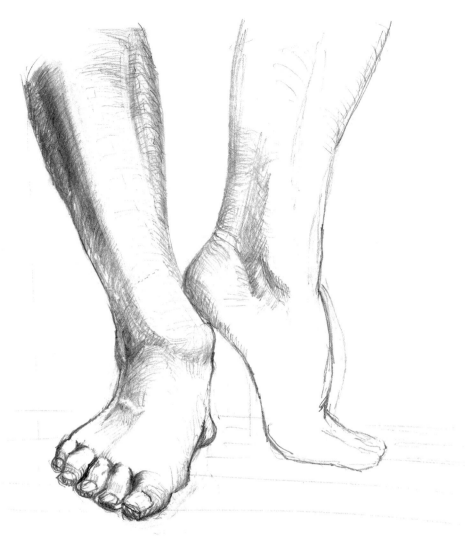

FIG 5.2 One of my preparatory life drawings

must have been done first of someone else's feet. To refresh my memory I also made a number of drawings of my own feet (Fig 5.2), basing them on photographs I had had taken in the pose, and elaborating on them by further inspection and touch. This is important when drawing or sculpting from life: you need to see many views to understand the one you are concentrating on. Drawing forces you to look, and the more you look, the more you notice and learn the shapes. As I have said elsewhere, you must think of your drawings as diagrams rather than pictures, and not despair if

what you produce is a mess. A much-revised drawing is a sign that you have been really looking.

Being able to feel any object is also informative, as it enables you to distinguish hard forms from soft and, in the case of a body, feel the direction of bones, tendons and muscles which may not be immediately obvious to the eye but which are essential to the shapes you see (Figs 5.3 and 5.4). It is also enormously useful to have a mirror propped up at an angle on the floor so you can see your feet all around.

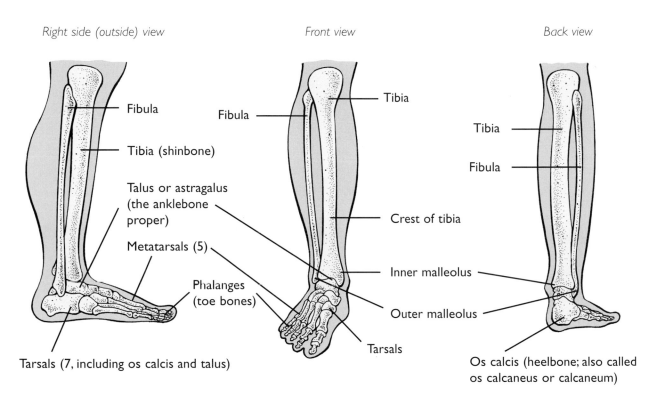

Right side (outside) view

Fibula

Tibia (shinbone)

Talus or astragalus
(the anklebone
proper)

Metatarsals (5)

Phalanges
(toe bones)

Tarsals (7, including os calcis and talus)

Front view

Fibula

Tibia

Crest of tibia

Inner malleolus

Outer malleolus

Tarsals

Back view

Tibia

Fibula

Os calcis (heelbone; also called
os calcaneus or calcaneum)

FIG 5.3 The bones of the right foot and lower leg

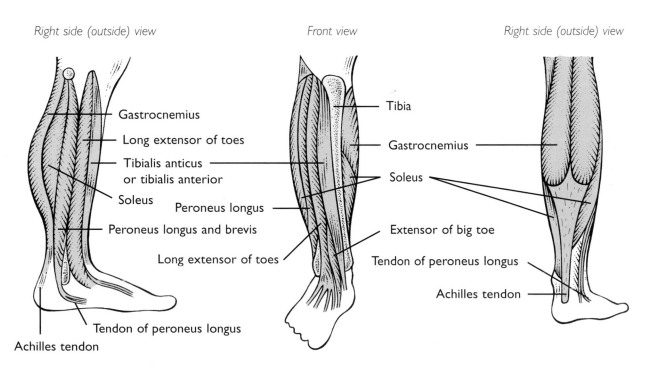

Right side (outside) view

Gastrocnemius

Long extensor of toes

Tibialis anticus
or tibialis anterior

Soleus

Peroneus longus and brevis

Tendon of peroneus longus

Achilles tendon

Front view

Tibia

Gastrocnemius

Soleus

Peroneus longus

Long extensor of toes

Right side (outside) view

Soleus

Extensor of big toe

Tendon of peroneus longus

Achilles tendon

FIG 5.4 The muscles of the right foot and lower leg

Choice of wood and grain direction

For this composition in life size you will need a piece of wood at least 12in (305mm) in two directions and about 10in (255mm) in the third. I used some of the same planewood as for the knees in Chapter 4. I placed the feet with the grain running vertically up the legs. As well as making the carving stronger, this is also visually more effective than having the stripes of the figure running horizontally across the legs.

The carving

I roughly chainsawed the waste off, keeping the larger offcuts to patch any shakes which could become a nuisance. I further shaped the feet with a wood-cutting disc on an angle grinder (Fig 5.5). I could, however, have done the whole carving with hand tools, only more slowly. I left a flat area around the feet for clamping purposes, which meant I could hold the wood flat on the bench or hold it on its side in a vice – although because this base consisted of end grain and had some bad

FIG 5.5 *The composition roughed out with chainsaw and angle grinder*

splits, it was not very strong. Later, when the heavy carving with the mallet had been completed on the upper parts of the sculpture, I screwed the block onto a small universal vice which enabled me to change its position quickly. Every carver will have his own ways of holding work, and some will have to manage with slower methods. I cannot stress enough that you must provide for holding the work firmly at all times.

Most of the carving is done with two deep gouges which are used to work around the forms, going across the grain. It is possible to follow a varying contour by raising the handle of the gouge as it goes into a dip and lowering the handle as it comes out of it. Successive cuts follow the contour, varying the character of the curves as the forms change in nature. For instance, there are hollows where muscles meet, and on each side of the Achilles tendon above its junction with the heelbone (**os calcis**, **os calcaneus** or **calcaneum**). This tendon is almost rope-like, with hollows on each side of varying shape and size from high up where the soleus muscle on the calf joins it, down to the sides of the heelbone.

It is possible to carve *along* the forms with flatter gouges instead, but there is a danger of missing the subtlety of the junctions between them. Eventually, of course, it will be necessary to smooth the surface with flatter tools: although the horizontal grooves caused by the deep gouges can be quite attractive and do indicate the nature of the curves, they do not reveal the shape of the foot any more clearly than a thick pair of socks does (Fig 5.6). Another benefit of carving around the forms is that there is no danger of working from profiles at right angles to each other, with the resulting square effect.

When carving a life-size copy, it is helpful to use a pair of callipers, but they must be used only for a few key measurements such as lengths of feet and toes, the height of the ankle bones, and the widths and thicknesses of the feet. As usual, do not try to measure everything, as it delays you and can make the carving unexciting for you – and hence for the viewer.

Elements to establish early are the slant of the shinbone from the middle of the leg to the inner malleolus (or what is commonly called the inner anklebone), and the relative positions of inner and outer malleolus (see Fig 5.3). (Strictly speaking the **talus** or **astragalus**, one of the **tarsals**, is the real anklebone, but it is hidden inside the joint.) The inner malleolus is higher up and further forward than the outer, and has no hollow in front of it.

The Achilles tendon and the back of the heel should also be marked, together with the width of the heel and the width of the foot at its widest, near the roots of the toes. All these data are best marked on with a generous allowance of wood, in case pieces come away by accident.

You will notice there is no attempt to create the hole between the feet nor the instep of the right foot until the outside shapes have been fixed (Fig 5.7). I have seen too many disasters caused by separating forms prematurely – although in this case I decided I did need to separate the calves of the legs early. The position of the heel of the left foot where it rests on the top of the inner malleolus of the right is crucial. One of the most difficult things in sculpture is carving two objects so they just touch. It is very easy to shape them so

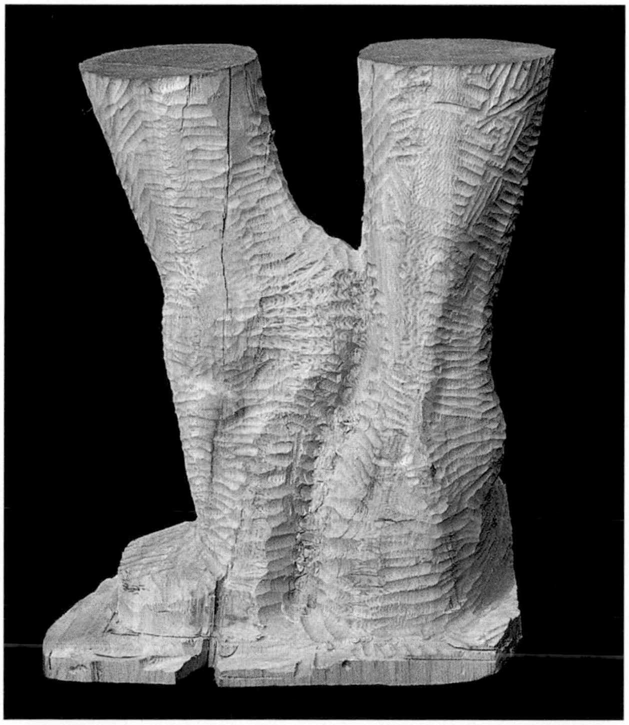

FIG 5.6 Most of the carving is done by cutting across the grain with deep gouges. Notice that, although the legs have been carved so that they are separated, there will be no gap between the feet until the outside shapes have been defined

FIG 5.7 Holes can be drilled through the space between the feet, but only once the outside shapes have been defined

thoroughly that they cease to touch, or leave them looking as if one is sunk into the other. There is not much flesh on top of the ankle or under the heel, so there should be little of the sinking-in effect, but each does slightly affect the shape of the other (Fig 5.8).

Apart from the bones of the toes, there are seven tarsal and five **metatarsal** bones in the body of the foot (Figs 5.9–5.11). Of these, you usually see only the heelbone. You can feel the others, but on merely looking at the foot it is virtually impossible to distinguish between the bumps they make and the blood vessels. However, if they were not there the foot would be as flaccid as a lump of wet dough. It is these bones that account for the wedge shape of the foot, and the fact that it is higher on the inner side of the arch than on the outside. It is the metatarsals that fan out to make the front of the foot wider than the heel.

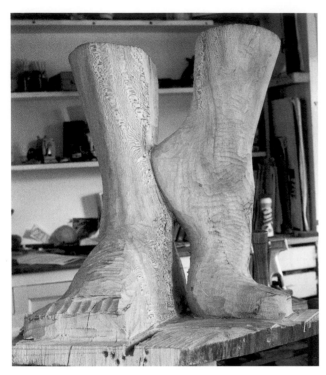

FIG 5.8 The left foot is almost finished, so the heel can now be carved pressing against the ankle of the right. Little give is present in either heel or ankle. Once the area of contact has been fixed, the hole beneath can be finished

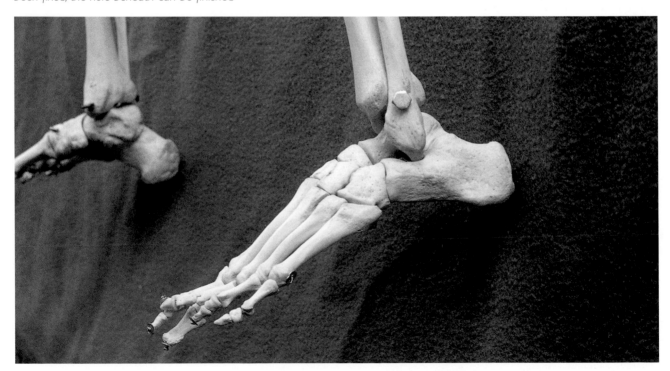

FIG 5.9 View of the bones of the left foot from the outside, with the inside of the right foot just visible. The inner malleolus is obviously further forward and higher than the outer

FIG 5.10 *The bones of the right foot from the inside. The arching of the foot means that only the bones belonging to the big toe and the second are visible*

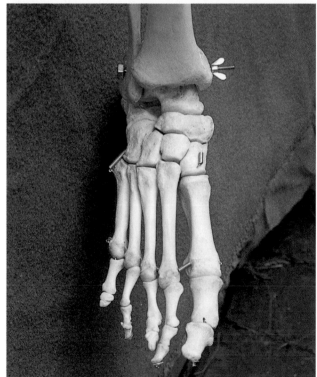

FIG 5.11 *The bones of the right foot from above. Note that all the toes have three phalanges, except the big toe which has only two (sometimes there are only two phalanges for the little toe, too). The relative heights of the inner and outer malleoli are visible*

Tendons

On top of the bones are the tendons. Apart from the very obvious Achilles tendon, there are the tendon of the **peroneus**, which runs down the outside of the ankle and swings around the outer malleolus and forwards (Fig 5.12), and the various tendons that run down the front of the leg. These are very powerful ones which you can see if you move your foot from side to side and put pressure on the toes. These tendons run along the tops of the tarsals and metatarsals to join the toes; they run in straight lines or in taut curves. They are also hard and, like the bones, affect the shape of the foot even when you think you cannot see them. In Fig 5.13 I have drawn attention on the left foot to those running down from the top of the foot at the ankle to the roots of the little and big toes.

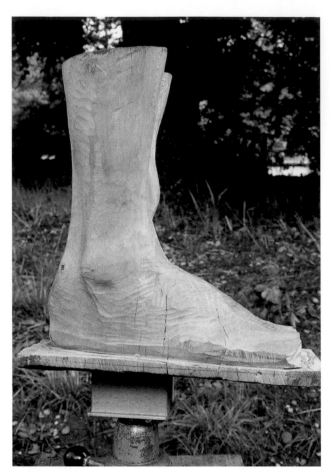

FIG 5.12 *The right foot, showing the tendon of the peroneus longus muscle pulling around the head of the outer malleolus (the lower head of the fibula)*

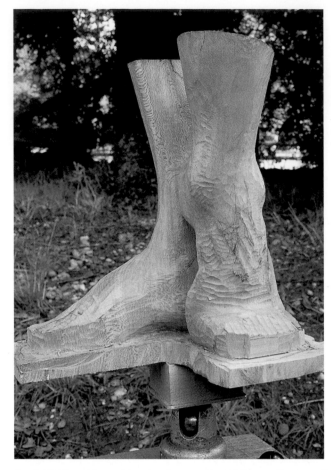

FIG 5.13 *The ridges of two tendons are just visible on the top of the right foot. On the left, the three diagonal ridges and a pencil line running across below them represent blood vessels. The tendons of the big and little toes are pencilled in above them*

Limiting surface detail

There are more creases and blood vessels than I have included. The danger of carving them all is that the surface detail detracts from the main forms. I have included the most prominent, hoping to show how the creases are in fact the grooves between folds of skin which are not necessarily continuous, and that blood vessels are not worm-like forms lying just under the skin or, even worse, on top of it. Blood vessels wander and do not push up the skin to the same extent on each side, or even in the same way along their length (Figs 5.14 and 5.15). It is useful

to begin by isolating these forms with shallow gouge or V-cuts on each side. The creases, however, are very consciously carved as convex folds, with varying kinds of convexity descending into the grooves. The blood vessels I treated in much the same way as the initial shaping of the legs, by working across the forms. The result is that you can see they are there, but they are no more obtrusive than in nature. The same treatment is used in carving the hand in Chapter 6. You will have noticed how the blood vessels in real life are more or less prominent when you are hot or cold, and how they stand out more on old people.

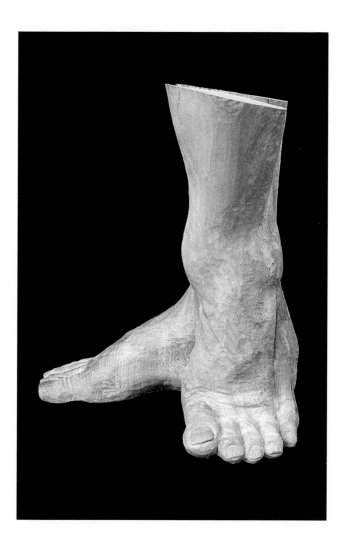

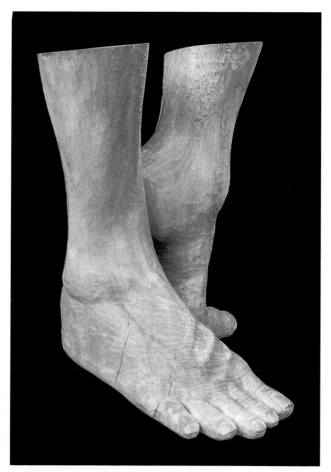

FIG 5.14 The finished carving: the front view of the left foot shows the blood vessels and gentle creases

FIG 5.15 The right foot from the outside, showing the tendon of the peroneus longus muscle passing behind the outer malleolus and, on top of the foot, some blood vessels crossing the tendons. Note the junctions between the toes and the rest of the foot

Toes

Toes cannot be carved until the rest of the foot is finished. If they are done beforehand, it is possible that they will not join convincingly to the feet without your having to recarve all your careful shaping. As with the creases and folds behind the toes of the left foot, a V-chisel may mark the divisions between the toes (Fig 5.16), but it should be noted the toes are not straight like little dowels, nor are the tops of the toes flat (Fig 5.17). They have knuckles, as do the fingers. Between the knuckles the toes are more rounded. Only when the knuckles and straighter sections are finished should the nails be carved. These could be outlined with a V-tool, but in this case, where the tops of the feet are in end grain, I used a no. 3 gouge with a rounded end. The wood broke off short at the back and sides of the nails. The join of

the flesh with the nail was then very easily shaped with various gouges, a small, shallow backbent being particularly useful.

Finishing

The bull-nosed no. 3 is a useful tool for general finishing. The corners, being rounded, do not dig in when carving into hollows. The bottoms of the hollows are completed by working across the grain with a gouge that fits the desired curvature as closely as possible. Because of the direction of the grain, and because the base impeded me, I used a large backbent near the bottom of the carving (Fig 5.18) and, for the junctions of the toes with the foot, a shortbent V-tool.

The scale of this carving is so big that it could be sanded without blurring the forms, but the chisel

FIG 5.16 Using a V-tool (parting tool) to begin the separation of the toes

FIG 5.17 Using a gouge with the hollow side down to round the top of a toe

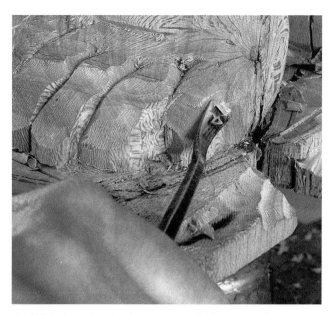

FIG 5.18 *A shallow backbent gouge facilitates cutting upwards on end grain near the bottom of the carving*

finish better suggests the imperfections of the natural surface (Figs 5.19 and 5.20), and will achieve uniformity when treated with raw linseed oil. These feet will be used as a teaching aid and so will not warrant a stone base, but they will need careful handling, since the toes are short-grained and vulnerable.

The ancient Romans used the image of reconstructing a complete sculpture of Hercules from just one foot ('ex pede Herculem'). It meant devising a theory or whole philosophy from a small fragment of evidence. If you carve a foot you may not have the foundation for a new philosophy, but you will have a sound basis for the next human figure you carve.

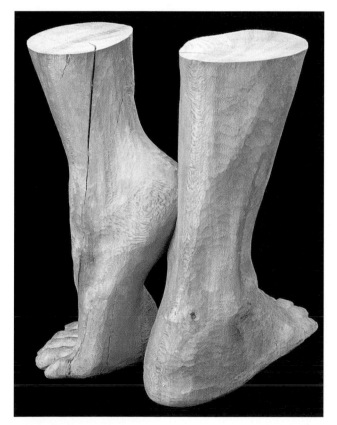

FIG 5.19 *The back view. Notice on the heel of the right foot that the prominence on the back of the os calcis is above ground level*

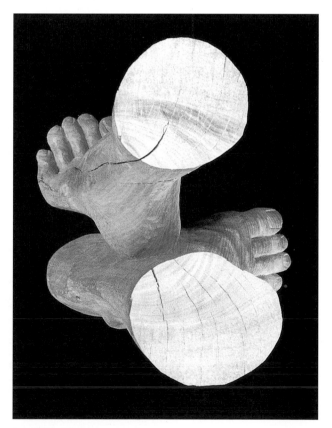

FIG 5.20 *The top view of the feet is a reminder that the legs are not square. On the right leg the hollow between the shinbone and the soleus/gastrocnemius group is very clear*

THE HAND AND ARM

Some people, when they see bricks, can think only of walls. Some see cars and can think only of transport. Yet each has texture, colour, mass and shape – attributes of sculpture. We see a hand and think of what it can do or what it might represent, but we seldom enjoy it as a shape in its own right. Elbows, too, are noticed little, yet contain fascinating shapes which you can learn, learn from

and enjoy by carving. Here the carving of the elbow and lower arm is completed by the hand, which is a commonly and often poorly carved subject (Fig 6.1).

The arm differs from the leg in that the elbow not only bends forwards but also allows the two lower bones to rotate around each other – which is why

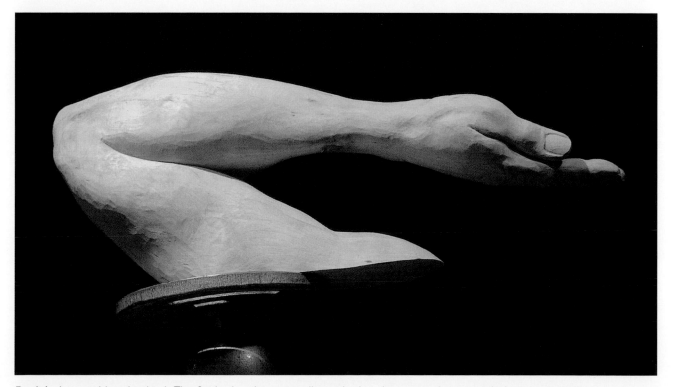

FIG 6.1 *Arm and hand in birch. The finished sculpture is still attached to the universal vice on which it was carved*

we can place our hands prone (face down), and supine (face up). Our feet, on the other hand, have little sideways movement. This means that the muscles and bones of the arm must be closely studied, as they can change so much. The composition chosen here draws attention to the bones of the elbow, exerts strain on the muscles and puts the hand in the prone position.

It is not easy to see your own elbow and the back of your upper arm, but unless you have a patient model you will need to use your own arms. For this exercise I did as with the previous projects: I had some photographs taken of my arm in the position I planned to carve, and then drew from them (Fig 6.2). It is also helpful to have a mirror in the workshop. Unless one arm is quite different from the other, you will find it easier to study in the mirror the opposite arm to the one you are carving. Another aid to carving is to take plaster casts of the arm and hand. The impression may not be absolutely accurate, but will be a guide.

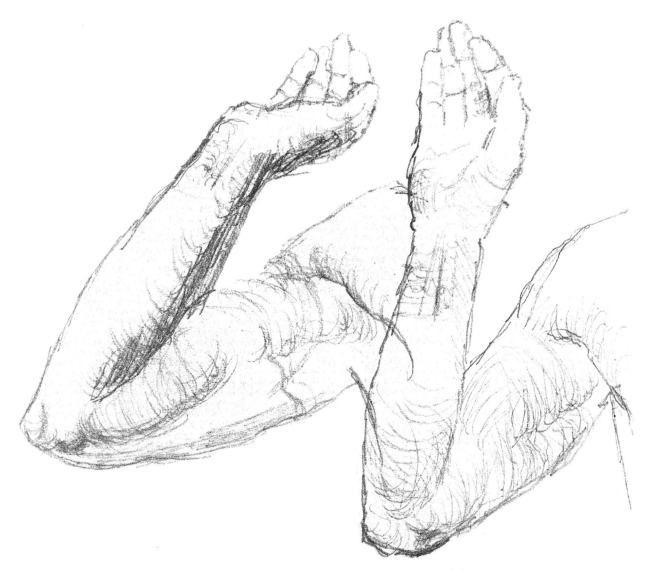

Fig 6.2 Some of my initial sketches, made using a mirror and photographs

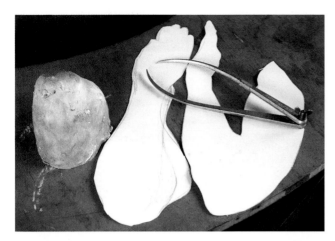

FIG 6.3 *Card templates, callipers and a plaster cast of the elbow used as aids before and during carving*

It is not 'cheating' to get someone to draw profiles round your arm onto card which you can use as templates for preparing your wood. As these may be inaccurate, allow a good margin round them when drawing onto the wood (Fig 6.3).

This arm is life-sized, which means I had to lose some of the upper arm to fit it into the available piece of wood. The composition was chosen to get the most out of the shape of the elbow. The hand is kept with the fingers slightly curved but together. Its position facing forwards changes the plane through the wrist and twists the muscles of the forearm in an interesting way.

I used birch (*Betula* sp.), which is seldom carved in Britain – possibly because of its reputation for breaking off short – but is much used in Scandinavia. It is paler than lime and has a fine, even texture and a pleasant lustre. My piece had developed shakes while drying, despite my painting the ends. But I had successfully protected it from mould, so there was no softening or staining. As this wood is one of the most prone to rot, as soon as it was felled I had painted it with disinfectant to kill fungus spores.

FIG 6.4 *The bandsawn block. Note that plenty of spare wood has been allowed, particularly around the wrist and hand*

I cut the wood to profile using the card templates (Fig 6.4), leaving a wide margin. I used a bandsaw to save time; if you do not have one, it is quite possible to cut the profiles by hand. I then used callipers to mark various basic measurements, and briefly rounded off the obvious corners with the angle grinder.

Probably the commonest mistake when carving or modelling arms is to forget the rigidity and the directions of the bones (Figs 6.5 and 6.6). In this pose the bump on the end of the elbow, the

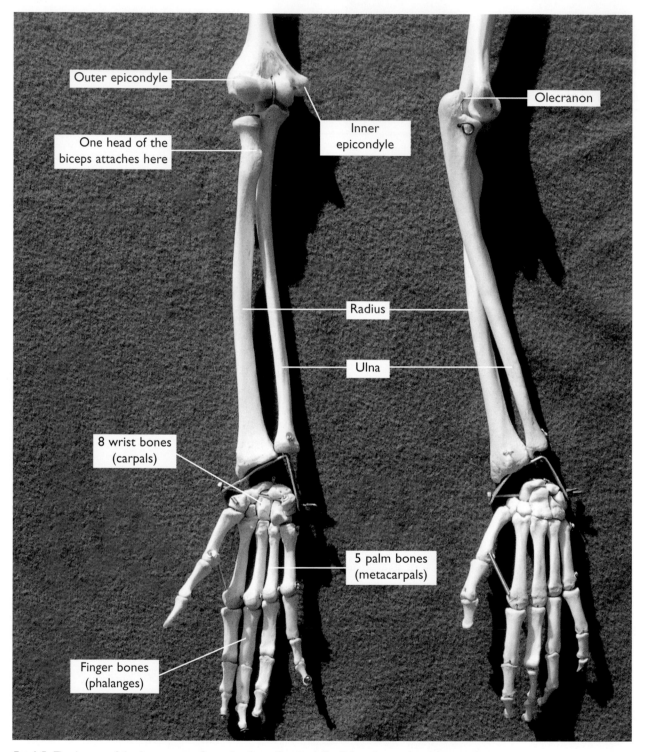

Outer epicondyle

Inner epicondyle

Olecranon

One head of the biceps attaches here

Radius

Ulna

8 wrist bones (carpals)

5 palm bones (metacarpals)

Finger bones (phalanges)

FIG 6.5 *The bones of the lower arms from the front. On the left of the picture the right arm has the hand facing forward. The left hand has been turned so that it faces backwards. Notice how the ulna rotates around the radius. One or two of the finger bones are facing the wrong way*

olecranon process of the ulna (which we call the funny bone), is visibly connected by a shallow groove with the ulna's head on the back of the wrist at the little finger side (Fig 6.7). The bumps which are visible on each side of the elbow are the inner and outer **epicondyles** of the upper arm bone or humerus (Figs 6.8 and 6.9). The other bone of the lower arm, the radius, is felt only at the wrist end and can be followed from its head, below the thumb, to the point where it disappears under the muscles of the forearm (Figs 6.10 and 6.11).

Muscles and tendons

The muscles are confusing, particularly when twisted as they are here, so should be copied from what you see. The muscles of the forearm are mainly concerned with operating the fingers, so they should be well developed on a carver. The tendons connecting them are channelled inside the transverse carpal ligament (the carpal tunnel) at the wrist. Some of them can be seen under the skin on the wrist, the back of the hand and the fingers, where they run through grooves in the knuckles.

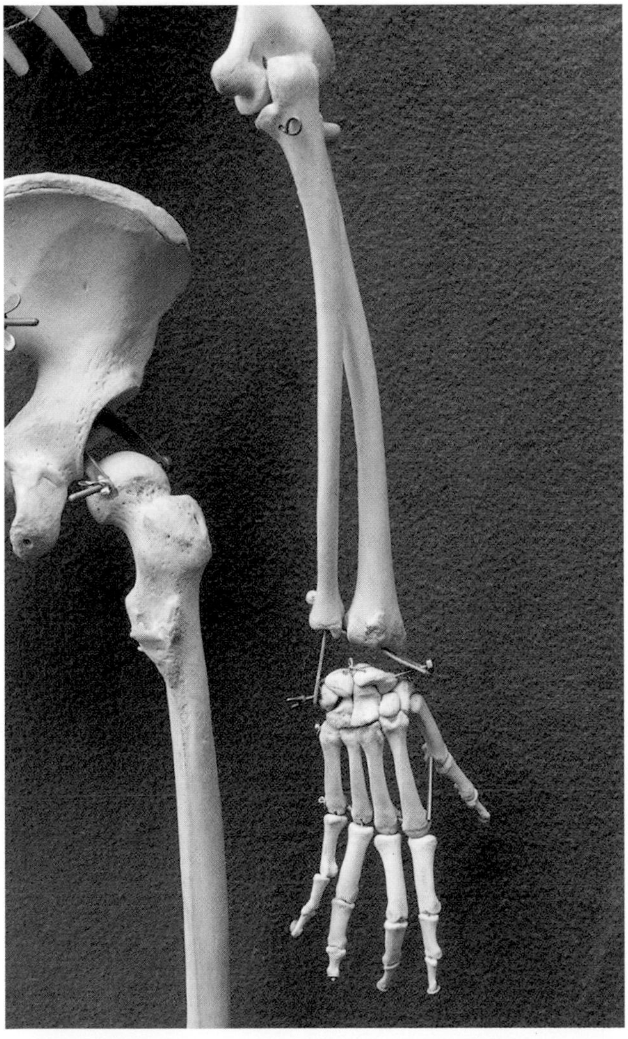

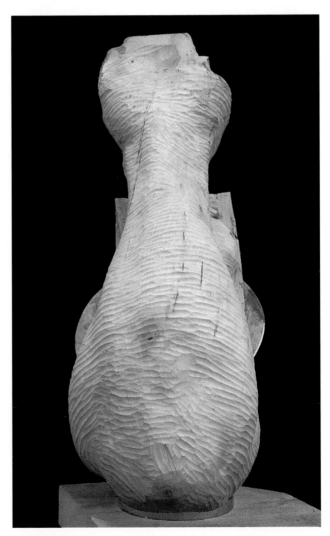

FIG 6.6 The lower right arm from behind. Note the olecranon process standing out in the middle of the elbow joint, and the distance that the fingertips reach down the thigh

FIG 6.7 The slight groove running along the edge of the ulna to its head at the wrist is seen on the left side of the roughed-out carving

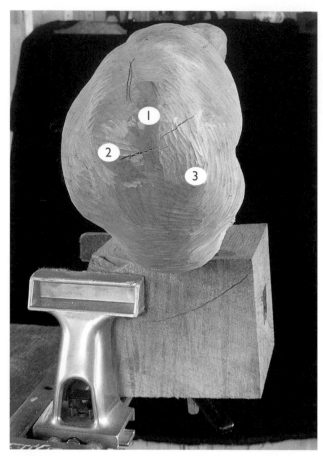

FIG 6.8 *The elbow joint seen end on, with the shapes of the bones beginning to emerge. 1 is the olecranon process or funny bone on the end of the ulna. 2 is the outer, 3 is the inner epicondyle of the humerus*

In contrast to the hard lumps and straight lines of tendons, and the more or less straight lines of bones, are the soft, rounded forms of muscles and fat. In this pose, the muscle groups on the front of the upper and fore arms are squeezed together to give beautiful curves which at the point where they meet on the inside angle turn very quickly and then flatten out on each side of a very tight crease (Fig 6.12). When carving, it is important to bear these hard and soft elements in mind, and to avoid separating groups of muscles and bones too abruptly.

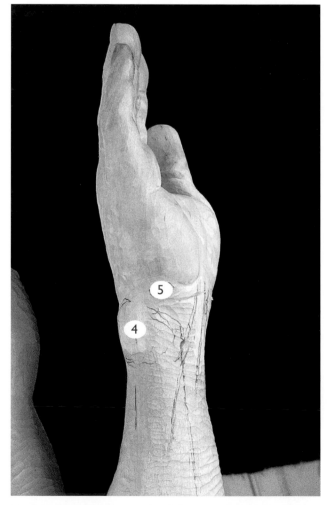

FIG 6.10 *The little finger side of the wrist. 4 is the head of the ulna nearest the hand; 5 is the **pisiform carpal**, one of the bones at the base of the palm*

FIG 6.9 *The bones of the elbow as they appear end on in the finished carving*

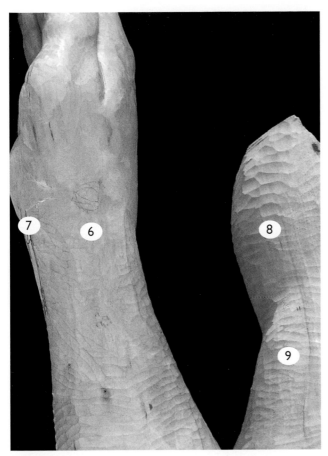

FIG 6.11 *The thumb side of the wrist. 6 is the* **styloid process** *of the radius. 7, just visible on the front of the wrist, marks the* **flexor carpi radialis**, *a prominent tendon on the inside of the wrist. 8 is the deltoid and 9 the biceps. With the lower arm rotated, the biceps does not bunch easily*

FIG 6.12 *This view of the finished arm shows the flat crease formed between the upper and lower arms*

Close examination of your own arm will show that forms tend to merge. For instance, where the ulna produces a slight hollow running from the elbow to the wrist, it is not the same hollow all the way. Muscles spread across it, almost flattening it out in one place (see Fig 6.7). The outlines may be carved along the forms with deep gouges or V-chisels, but I prefer to work around the forms with a no. 9 gouge about ⁹⁄₁₆in (14mm) wide. Sometimes I first make a hollow for the waste wood to break into, but, in order to concentrate on the qualities of curves and how they vary, I usually make the chisel fall and rise across gently undulating forms, as with the carvings in previous chapters. You have to remember that the bottom of the channel left by the chisel must not be lower than the intended final surface. If at least one corner of the gouge is kept out of the wood, the risk of splitting what you want to keep is much reduced.

Making the carving readable from a distance

When carving anything from life, it is important to check, when you think you have succeeded, whether the hollows are deep enough to read clearly. It is more sculptural to exaggerate. If you work around rather than along the forms, you should lose the squareness which tends to result if you work from profiles.

The hand

I carved the arm first, partly to make it easier to work on the back of the hand, but mainly to ensure the hand joined it convincingly (Fig 6.13). Held like this, the palm of the hand forms quite a deep cup, so it is wise to begin by getting close to

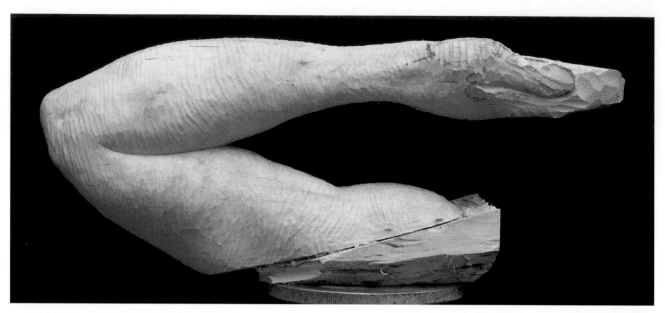

FIG 6.13 *The hand is begun only when the arm has been fully shaped. A saw cut marks the waste wood at the top of the arm which will eventually be removed*

FIG 6.14 *The palm of the hand is rounded to form the cup. Plenty of thickness has been allowed for the fingers. The fingertips have been cut as steps, but no attempt is yet made to divide the fingers*

FIG 6.15 *The knuckles are marked on the back of the hand*

the final shape of the back and sides (Fig 6.14). It is tempting to cut the grooves between the fingers immediately, but the danger is that you produce rigid rods, strings of sausages or bananas.

Once the overall shape is formed, which you can check by looking at your own hand from all aspects in a mirror, you can start to make the

grooves. Even if the fingers are to be separate, they should still be shaped as one form to begin with (Fig 6.15). If the hand is life-size, you can lay your own hand on it to mark off the widths and shapes

98

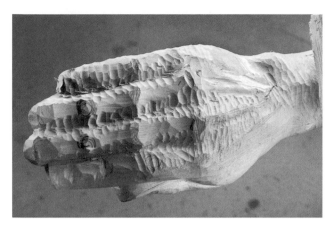

FIG 6.16 *The fingers and tendons on the back of the palm are formed by carving across them*

of the fingertips and the positions of the knuckles. Because of the tendons, the plane between the knuckles and the wrist is more or less straight, but there is considerable curvature from side to side, particularly near the base of the thumb. Allowance should be made for blood vessels if you are including them. As I carved this in a cool winter workshop, my blood vessels were not strongly marked, but showing one or two makes for realism (Fig 6.16).

Shaping the fingers

I outlined the blood vessels, tendons and fingers in the same way, by carving across them with a no. 4 gouge ¼in (6mm) wide, cutting across the grain, rising and falling over the forms. Only when it was impossible to bring the gouge up again from the bottoms of the grooves between fingers without digging into the opposite rise did I use a V-chisel or the edge of a ½in (13mm) bull-nosed no. 3 (Swiss no. 2) gouge, slid along like a knife (see Fig 6.18). This ensures the right sort of curve is given to each part of each finger, and avoids making them rigid. Think not of carving the grooves, so much as of shaping the individual fingers.

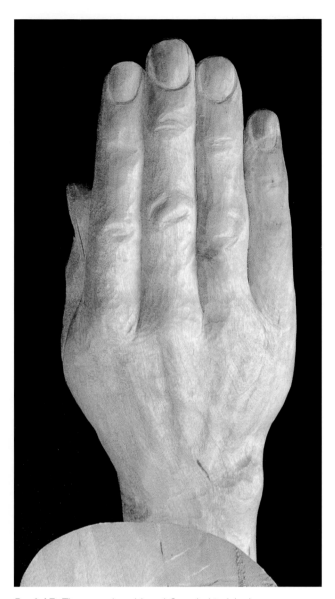

FIG 6.17 *The completed hand from behind. It does not seem wrong that there are no holes between the fingers. The blood vessels, tendons and nails make it look realistic. The chiselled finish gives an impression of flesh*

It helps to keep the fingers touching. For a carving to look good, holes or other negative spaces should make important shapes and not be just slots or gaps. Even though in this pose daylight is visible between the fingers, the holes are not helpful except to the literal-minded who think there should be no difference between a carving in wood and a real hand (Fig 6.17).

On the front, the fingers are separated in the same way as on the back; but, whereas on the back they are divided into knuckles and **phalanges** with tendons and muscles on them, on the front they are more fleshy with at least one crease where they bend on the inside of each joint (Fig 6.18). These creases seldom run in regular straight lines. The inside of the hand has many rounded cushion shapes separated by deep furrows. Whichever way these furrows are made, make sure the forms between them are deeply rounded into them.

Finishing techniques

A little-known tool which is useful for carving the lines of the palm and between the fingers is the wing parting tool. It is available from Pfeil, the Swiss maker, as shape no. 22, and from Henry Taylor as no. 47; I believe Ashley Iles will make them to order. Resembling a V-tool made from two inverted shallow gouges, this tool cuts grooves which are rounded up from the bottom.

Fortunately my hands reflect my age, so the skin is not as tight as when I was young. This means a chisel finish is more lifelike. In any case, no one's skin is as smooth and shiny as sandpapered wood. But if you do not have enough tools to fit all the shapes, abrasive paper could be used, particularly if the form is stylized and the carving is in a hard wood. I normally object to abrasives, as they blur the forms, deaden the surface and are tedious to use. There were some whiskers left on my carving, which I wiped off by lightly papering

FIG 6.18 Carving the grooves between the fingers on the inside of the hand using a bull-nosed no. 3 gouge

with 400-grit paper. On a heavily tooled surface this takes down the high points and leaves the bottoms of cuts a different colour. Oiling the wood reduces the effect, and exposure to light blends it all together. In this case I used one coat of Danish oil; linseed oil might have made it look too yellow.

As this piece is copied fairly accurately, it verges on model making. It is elevated above this by concentrating on the contrasts between hard and soft and the directions of bones and tendons, without any obsessive accuracy of finish (Fig 6.19). A century ago this would have been accepted as sculpture, but now if offered to some art galleries it would be dismissed as craft unless it were placed in some telling context such as emerging from an engine or hanging in a butcher's shop. Its final situation is on the ceiling above where I often sit (Fig 6.20).

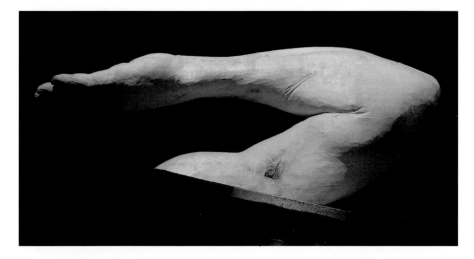

FIG 6.19 *The finished arm. The chiselled finish is barely noticeable*

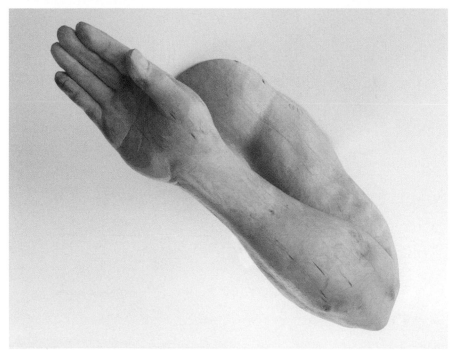

FIG 6.20 *The 'Hand of God' attached to the ceiling*

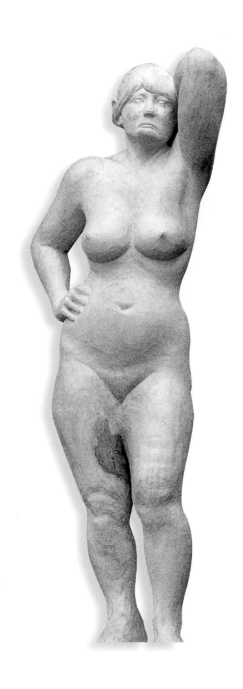

CARVING THE WHOLE FIGURE

It is usually easier to see the bone and muscle formations on a man's body (Fig 7.1) than on a woman's, so we have so far studied the anatomy by carving the separate parts of a man's body. Now, however, the parts are employed all together to show how they relate to one another. I have chosen to demonstrate this by discussing the carving of a female nude (Fig 7.2). The body of a

FIG 7.1 *The Inlooker in Portland stone. Because it was carved long ago, this life-sized piece has acquired some lichen and been slightly eroded by acid rain. The bones and muscles are strongly marked. If I did this piece now I should allow more stone for the hair*

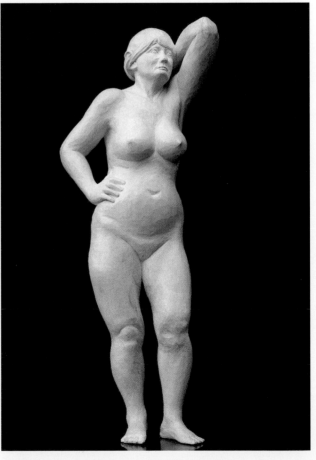

FIG 7.2 *Nude female figure carved in sycamore*

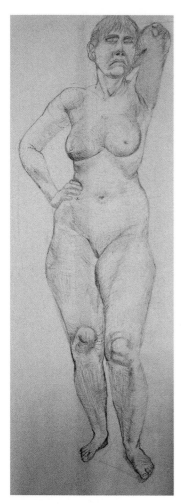

FIGS 7.3–7.5 Drawings from life model. Note the perspective in the lower legs and feet, also the ways used to indicate qualities of curve

woman is probably more often sculpted than a man's, and its differences need to be explained.

Among the earliest sculptural images are the voluptuous so-called Venus figures with their exaggerated middle portions and breasts. Perhaps the carvers preferred a different style of model from today's. Perhaps that is what women looked like then. Most likely the carvers were developing those forms that distinguish the female from the male, namely those aspects of female anatomy associated with fertility. For them the carved figure probably had some ritual power. For us the

female figure is used in sculpture as part of a story or allegory, or simply as an object for admiration because of the beauty of its shapes. As with any carving, the stronger the artist's feelings are about it, the better the sculpture will be.

Whereas the primitive carver seems all too aware of the essence of the female form, there have been periods when the artist – possibly because he was a monk and therefore not able to see the naked female form for himself – carved his women with men's bodies, apart from the obvious omission, but with wider hips, and breasts stuck on like upturned pudding basins. Even Michelangelo was not immune from this. The women's pubic hair, where included, was sometimes developed upwards in a point, a feature more common in men.

I carved the figure shown in this chapter as a demonstration piece rather than to illustrate a story. She is doing nothing except standing upright in an apparently pensive pose, but she does show what happens to shoulders, breasts and hips when one arm is raised and one leg is bent, with the weight being carried on the other. The arms are away from the body so that the shapes of the ribcage are accessible, and each arm and shoulder is shaped differently because of its position. The head is turned slightly to one side, looking upwards, to show how this affects the shapes of the front of the neck and to illustrate the problems which arise when one tries to carve a turned head.

Preparing for the carving

First I drew a live model from four different viewpoints (Figs 7.3–7.5 show three of them) and made some additional studies of the feet. It is tempting to think that photographs will supply all the information you need. However, unless the lighting is very carefully controlled much of the important shape is missed. Even views from above and below, unless recorded extremely thoroughly, are insufficient. Drawings enable you to record more fully, with your own diagrammatic style, much of the variety of shape. Drawing also helps you to leave out unnecessary details. However, although photographs, unlike drawings, do not force you to see, they are useful references. Although I did not make a maquette here, it would have been an excellent way of recording the subject.

It is important to remember when working from both drawings and photographs that perspective distorts. For instance, if your eye is level with the middle of the subject when you draw or photograph it, the figure will be increasingly foreshortened towards the head and feet. Notice particularly the perspective in the legs and feet in the drawings. Foreshortening must be compensated for when the outlines of the figure are drawn on the wood.

Choice of wood

For this exercise I used a log of green sycamore (*Acer pseudoplatanus*). When green it is very easy to carve and if, as in this case, the finished sculpture is nowhere very thick, it is unlikely to develop shakes. To prevent its splitting during the carving, I covered it with plastic when it was not being worked. Although the log had been treated with fungicide soon after felling, some mould staining had occurred, which meant that I had to treat the finished carving with a special wood bleach.

From my drawings I chainsawed it to a rough outline and followed this with an angle grinder equipped with an Arbortech Industrial cutting disc (Figs 7.6 and 7.7). Both remove bulk quickly, but as they can take away more than intended I soon resorted to chisels.

Learning and maintaining the proportions

The size of the head needs to be decided quickly, as by using its height one can quickly find the middle point of the body and identify other fixed points. The human head goes on average 7½ times into the total height of a standing adult. The result is that the midpoint, just above the fork of the legs

FIG 7.6 *The block of sycamore roughed out with chainsaw and Arbortech*

FIG 7.7 *Further roughing out done with the angle grinder; the first chisel cuts can also be seen. The darker yellow in places shows how the green wood has reacted quickly to air and light. The grey colour is caused by the use of disinfectant to prevent mould growth while the wood was wrapped in plastic to slow moisture loss*

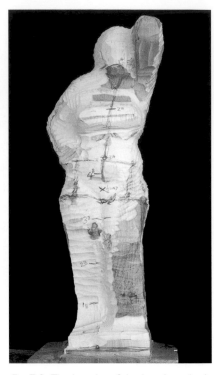

FIG 7.8 *The lengths of the head marked off on the body. 1A is the bottom of the chin. 3A is just below the navel. The middle of the body is about 3¾ heads from the top and from the bottom. 1B to 4B are head lengths from the underside of the feet. The tilt between the furthermost forward parts of the pelvis and between the great trochanters is marked with a pencilled rectangle to show that the two lines remain parallel*

– about the top of the pubic hair on a woman – is 3¾ head-lengths from both the crown of the head and the sole of the foot. The size of the head may in fact be varied. The ancient Greeks tended to make it one-eighth of the total height. Medieval carvers often made it one-ninth, to make the figure look taller. The lengths of the head may be marked off on the body to help fix positions of nipples, navel and knees (Fig 7.8). The relative measurements of other parts of the body should be noticed, such as widths of shoulders and hips, lengths of upper and fore arms, thighs and lower legs (Fig 7.9). My carving is about one-third life size, so getting the proportions was comparatively easy. However, it is unlikely that your model will be prepared to pose in your workshop while you carve. As you will inevitably find that you have not taken some obviously essential measurement, you must in the end rely on your judgement. When establishing the positions of various parts of the body, a plumb line and a pair of callipers are useful. The plumb line will help determine the relative positions of top of sternum, navel, crutch and inside of thigh and ankle.

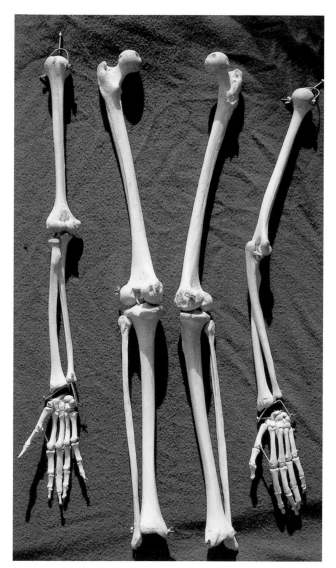

FIG 7.9 The lengths of the bones of the arms compared with those of the legs (the leg bones are seen from behind)

Once these main points are marked, the figure should be worked all together. In this case, however, because I needed strength in the legs while applying great force in carving the upper parts, I left most of the carving of the legs until the rest was done (Fig 7.10). I was aware that there was a diseased knot in the legs, but it was not until much later that I discovered how crumbly it was on the back of the legs, especially on the inside of the right thigh where the cut end of a branch can be clearly seen

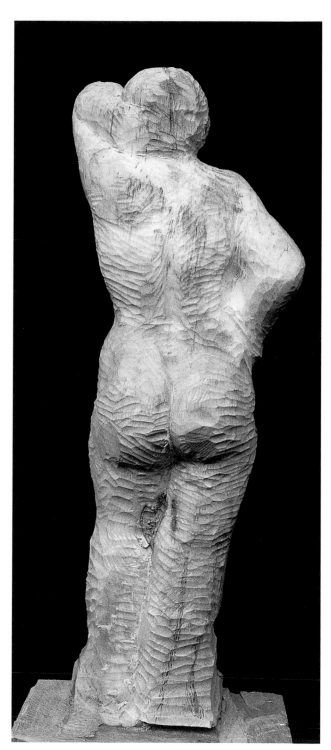

FIG 7.10 The main volumes and planes are worked in. The left shoulder blade is established. The tilt of the buttocks coincides with the tilt of the pelvis in Fig 7.8. The dead knot in the legs becomes evident. Note that the spaces between arms and body are not pierced, although they are gradually being worked up to

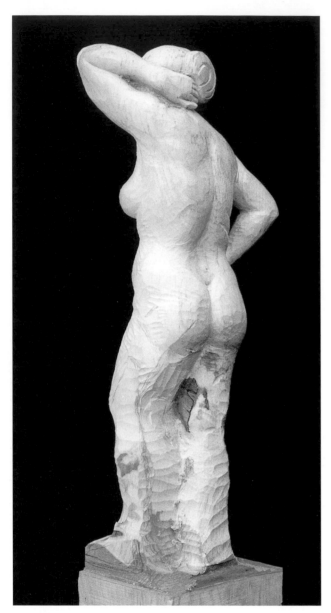

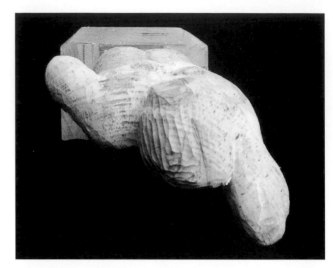

FIG 7.12 *The top of the head, showing the essential centre line. There is no squareness about the arms and ribcage. The left buttock is slightly further forward than the right*

FIG 7.11 *Although the legs are not so far developed as the body, their directions are already clear. The full extent of the dead knot is still not revealed. The flat cut end of the branch tells what has happened to cause the rot*

FIG 7.13 *The centre line continues down to the chin to show the tilt of the head. The line through the middle of the eyes is at right angles to it. The sterno-cleido-mastoid muscles are beginning to be carved*

(Fig 7.11). Incidentally, this shows that I am carving the log with the direction of the growing tree reversed; I have never found this to make any difference. This dead knot proved so troublesome that at the end of the carving I replaced it with one of the offcuts that I had kept against such an eventuality (see Figs 7.15 and 7.16).

As with any carving, the top view should be considered all the time. A centre line is drawn from the nape of the neck over the head and down to the chin (Figs 7.12 and 7.13). A line is also marked across the centre of the eyes. Both lines should be constantly redrawn to ensure that the slight tilts of the head sideways and upwards are

FIG 7.14 Top view of the back, showing the pressure of the left arm against the hair, the different shapes of the shoulder blades and the way the sacrum begins to turn into the top of the cleft of the buttocks

maintained. Before the face is roughed out the sides of the head should be shaped – allowing for hair and ears. It is easy to forget that the face is not square with the body. Always check that in your roughing out of the head you look at it square and

forget the attitude of the rest of the body. The only noticeable asymmetry in the shape of the head occurs where the hair is irregular because of the way it is dressed, and where the left arm and hand are touching it (Fig 7.14; see also Fig 7.17).

CARVING THE HUMAN FIGURE

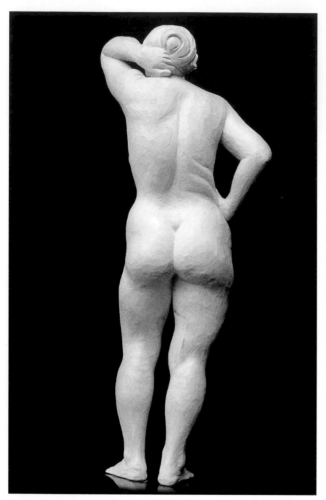

FIG 7.15 *The back view of the finished sculpture, showing the tilt of the hips and the little triangle at the top of the cleft of the buttocks; note how the pose gives rise to differences in the shoulder blades, the fleshiness of the backs of the knees and the Achilles tendons. The mould stains on the wood have been bleached away, and the dead knot replaced with an offcut*

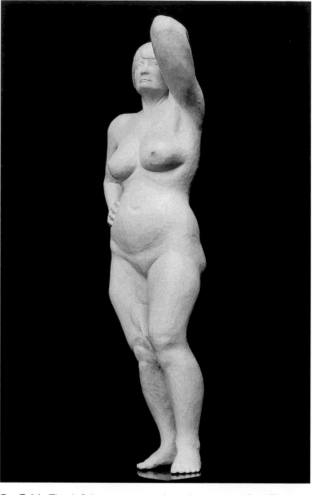

FIG 7.16 *The left breast is raised as the arm is lifted. The pectoral muscle can be seen running up onto the top of the arm at the shoulder. The kneecap on a woman tends to sink in more than on a man's leg*

The effects of bending one leg and raising one arm

The other areas of irregularity in the body are the obvious ones such as the positions of the arms and legs. At least as important are the relative heights of the shoulders when seen from behind, the shapes of the shoulder blades and buttocks (Fig 7.15) and the heights of the nipples and the points of the anterior iliac crests (Fig 7.16). These points

on the pelvis and the top ends of the thighbones (the great trochanters) form a rectangle, as we saw in Fig 7.8. When one leg is straight and the other bent, the pelvis on the side of the bent leg tilts out at the top and in at the bottom, while on the other side – in this case the right – the iliac crest moves inwards and the great trochanter moves out. This happens because the right leg is rigid to carry the weight, but the left side of the pelvis sags. In the small of the back there are often two dents visible

110

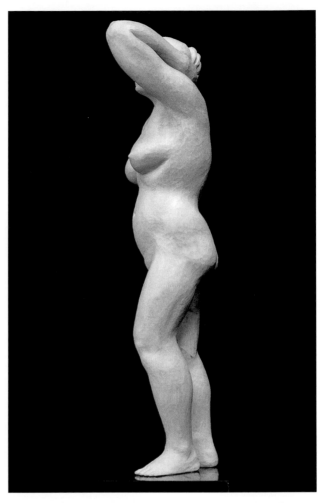

FIG 7.17 There is just enough detail in the hair and ear to make it clear that the strand over the ear represents hair. Some direction is given to the hair by means of cuts made with a broad, shallow gouge. Note how the fingers and thumb of the right hand sink into the flesh of the flank and abdomen. The hollow down the right thigh is quite different from that on the left thigh in the next photograph

FIG 7.18 Compare the thigh and hip with the right side in the previous photograph. Because the pelvis is tilted, the iliac crest pushes the gluteus medius towards us on the left side, creating a hollow under it

at the side points of the diamond-shaped hollow where the sacrum joins the pelvis; these tilt in the same direction. These were not visible on my model, but the tops of the buttocks do tilt (see Fig 7.15). In addition to the relative positions of the nipples, the breasts behave differently. When the breasts are small, the one under the raised arm may appear almost flat. In this case, the right breast hangs down and slightly outwards as it rests

on the ribcage, whilst the left breast is more rounded and faces more forward as the pectoral muscle on which it sits is pulled inwards by the raising of the arm. The thigh muscles also behave differently. The right leg is in tension, and so the muscles on the outside of the thigh (Fig 7.17) create hollows which do not appear on the left thigh, where the flesh tends to hang more softly around the bone (Fig 7.18).

The differences between male and female forms

It is instructive to contrast the male with the female form (Figs 7.19–7.21). A woman naturally has more reserves of fat, which are typically distributed on the buttocks, hips, thighs and nape of the neck, as well as softening the lines of the muscles on the arms, legs and torso, and on the face of a younger woman. The knees on a woman also differ from a man's (compare Figs 7.2, 7.16 and 7.17 with Figs 4.12 and 4.18). The sterno-cleido-mastoid muscles, on the other hand, which run from the junction of the collar bones with the sternum to the mastoid process on the skull just behind the ears, are more prominent on a woman because men tend to have thicker necks. In spite of my model's womanly shape, she is a regular games player and is very fit. Other models will have a different distribution of fat and, indeed, different proportions in their bone structure (Fig 7.22).

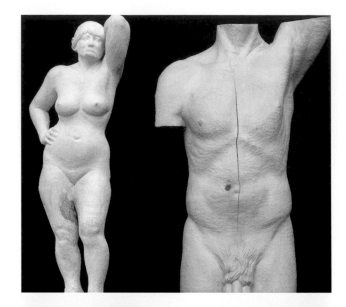

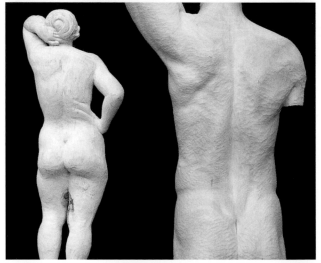

FIGS 7.19–7.21 The female figure compared with the male torso of Chapter 3. The differences in musculature and fleshy covering are clear. The external oblique muscle on the male forms a strong line where it rests over the iliac crest. The serratus muscles on the side of the ribcage, sloping from the bottom front edge of the thorax towards the armpit, were so faint on the female model that there was no point in including them. In the front view, the lower parts of the pectoral muscles on the left sides appear different because the woman's are affected by the roundness of the breast; where they travel up to the shoulder they are virtually the same. The back view shows the woman's wider hip and the fleshiness of the back, the deeper hollows in the small of the back and at the top of the cleft of the buttocks. The depressions at the sides of the buttocks are in the same place but rounder and softer on a woman. Note how the creases under the buttocks fade out into the thighs at the sides. Since the photographs in Chapter 3 were taken, a large split has developed down the front of the male torso, despite its having been hollowed; this has subsequently been filled with a well-dried offcut from the original log

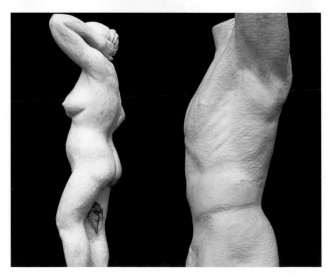

FIG 7.22 A cast in marble plaster of a copy of an ancient Greek stone figure. Note the slender but still rounded female form. The support for the legs separates from the body behind the knees with the result that the plaster, which has the same weaknesses as stone, has broken at the first weak point up the legs

As with carving a male figure, the bone structure must be remembered at all times. The principal difference between male and female lies in the woman's generally wider pelvis. The wider this is, the more the thighbones slope inwards to the knees. The hollow of the small of the back is also greater. In other respects the bones of both sexes are alike for our purposes. The ribcage is still there, causing the breasts to tilt slightly outwards and creating dents in the front of the body just about level with the navel

to form the waist, in the interval between the ribcage and the pelvis. The shoulder girdle formed by the collarbones and shoulder blades still floats around the ribcage and attaches the arms to it. The spine still forms a groove from neck to sacrum, showing bends only at the waist and neck; any other apparent curves in a normal spine are the result of different tensions of the muscles of the back. Like most women my model has a pad of fat over the seventh cervical vertebra – the lowest of the movable vertebrae of the neck.

Planning the order of carving

Following my general rule that it is not safe to carve hollows or holes until the outside shapes are worked out, the piercing between the arms and the body should be left until you know how much wood you have to spare. This means that for a long time the right arm appears to be very short. Incidentally, the upper right arm is about as near to a cylinder as any part of the human can be, but even here there are bumps, hollows and flats that indicate bone and muscle (Fig 7.23). One of the reasons why the right arm appears too short in the earlier photographs is that allowance has been made for the hand to actually press into the flesh on top of the iliac crest (see Figs 7.2 and 7.17). It is very important to include such touches as indicate the softness of flesh, as well as those which show muscles hardened by tension.

When carving the head, keep the face narrow and sloping well back from the nose to the back of the eye socket, and even more from the mouth and chin to the back of the jawbone. It is inadvisable to carve between the nose and the top of the upper lip or between the mouth and the chin for a long time, and the separation of the lips is best left to

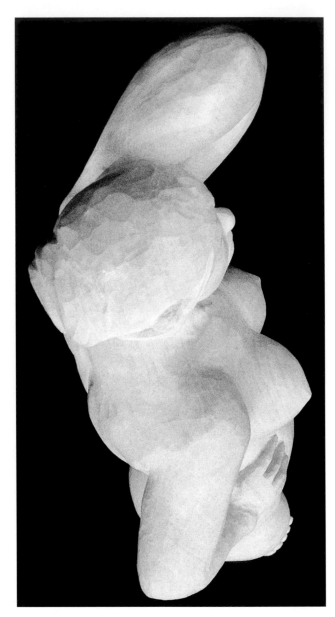

FIG **7.24** *The eyes in the process of being carved; at this stage they still join the eyebrow in the middle. Note the slope back to the outside corner of the eye and the slope back from cheek, mouth and chin to the back of the jaw*

makes carving the left side of the face difficult. It is in this and other similar positions that the greenness of the timber is useful, as it is possible to carve against the grain. Seasoned lime (*Tilia* x *europaea*) will generally let you do this, too.

The finish

As with the eyelids, it seems unnecessary to do more than indicate finger and toe joints and nails. Only slight detail is given to the hair (see Fig 7.17), although the strand passing across the ear needs some movement in it to distinguish it from a headband. The overall finish is straight from the chisel. After replacing the rotten wood and bleaching to remove mould stains, I covered the piece with a thin coating of a clear microcrystalline wax ('Renaissance Wax') and screwed it to a black marble base.

near the end. The eyeballs are carved by making deep hollows between them and the bridge of the nose and at the outer edges of the orbits, leaving a virtual column between the eyebrows and the cheek for the eye itself (Fig 7.24). I did not even detail all the eyelids. The effect is there without this and, in fact, to put them in all the way around each eye can make the eyes seem too small. The left arm

Carving the figure in stone

The same shapes are possible in stone but, because of its brittleness, and because it lacks the great strength that wood has along the grain, slender forms usually need supporting. If the sculpture is to be located well out of the reach of rough treatment and the violence of the weather, delicate parts may be safe. In the stone figure of the man shown here (Figs 7.1 and 7.25) there are no vulnerable projections. The arms are strong enough because they are attached at both ends. If you tackle a standing figure it is usual to provide support for the ankles, as they are the weakest part – although in the example shown in Fig 7.22 the legs above the support have not been strong enough.

Whichever medium you use, when you have carved two or three figures you will find you can improvise – although for every change of posture you will need to make further studies because of the various ways the bones and muscles behave and react to the surfaces they press against.

FIG 7.25 The Inlooker *from behind. Because the figure is bent forwards, the spines of the vertebrae stand out. The arms are surprisingly robust because they are touching the legs*

THE DRAPED FIGURE

The first thing to remember when carving a draped figure is that, whatever form the clothing takes, its shape is dictated by the figure underneath. Furthermore, the kinds of material that are suitable for clothing the human figure all tend to behave in the same way, so that whether you wear fur, leather, or textiles you find the same sorts of folds and creases.

The uses of drapery

In sculpture, however, drapery is usually used not merely as covering for the figure (Fig 8.1), but as part of the composition. Like the lines used by a cartoonist to indicate movement, the folds and swirl of drapery help us to read the sculpture (Fig 8.2).

In the Western tradition the uses and interpretation of drapery have changed not just with fashions in dress, but with perception of the figure and the forms of drapery. From the early Greek sculptures derived from Egyptian models to those of the Roman Empire, drapery developed from being highly stylized – merely an indication of clothing – to extreme realism which showed even the creases left after the material had been taken out of its storage chest. Later it returned to a

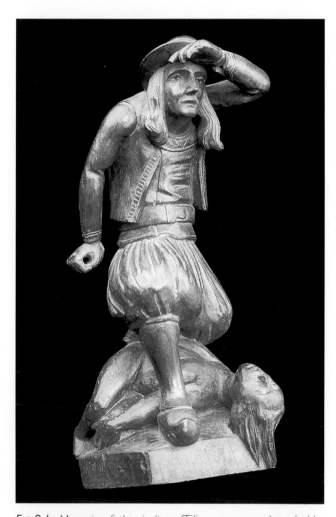

FIG 8.1 *Mourning father in lime (Tilia x europaea), probably early twentieth-century Breton. The drapery is merely representing dress – no attempt is made to exploit it for pattern or dramatic effect – although the style of hair and clothing is appropriate to a subject of droopy weariness*

The main form taken by drapery on early Greek and early medieval figures was the long fold. The folds were shown as rounded ridges and grooves. In some early or naïve pieces these pay no attention to the forms beneath; some even behave in an absurd way. Alternatively, in ancient Greece and Egypt the edges of drapery were sometimes merely drawn on the surface of a nude figure, with an allowance for a skirt.

What we can see in the better examples is that the drapery follows a deliberate pattern, which may simply decorate (Fig 8.3), but at best gives importance and grandeur to the figure. What we also see, in some pieces in archaic Greece and in medieval Europe when artists unaccustomed to realistic representation are at work, is that drapery does undraperylike things. Fluted folds follow a leg even when it is bent double, instead of following gravity. The concertina effect you sometimes find on a bent elbow is employed all over the arms and torso. Although these symbolize drapery, and even form attractive patterns, other contemporary examples show that drapery could be used to add movement, dignity and character.

FIG 8.2 Man in a wind, in wenge (Millettia laurentii), copied by the late David Wilson from a photograph of a sculpture by Ernst Barlasch. The movement of the drapery explains why the man is clutching his hat

simplified form. A similar development occurred again from the Dark Ages to the twentieth century.

After the Roman Empire not only did the carvers lose the skill, but their masters were mainly in the church. The church's message was simple, and even if there had been the opportunity and the skill available to make more realistic figures, the spirit of the time required easily understood symbols. Figures tended to be elongated, faces flattened, eyes large; and drapery was usually just a surface decoration, often hanging in long parallel folds.

FIG 8.3 This stretching man in oak (Quercus robur) on an early sixteenth-century misericord corbel from Vendôme, France, illustrates how drapery can be used to make a strong, simple pattern

Preliminary studies

Before beginning a carving, it is a good idea to study the ways drapery behaves: not only by drawing the clothed form but also by investigating, through studies of a piece of draped cloth, how fabric hangs and how it breaks when its fall is interrupted. A piece of fairly heavy material – blanket, velvet or canvas – is better than thin cotton which, if copied too closely, can look like crumpled paper. (You may wish to create this effect, but in general it distracts the eye and can look messy. It certainly has less chance of emphasizing the repose or the movement of a figure.)

Some drawings done from nature in this way, followed by some studies of draped sculpture, preferably in different styles, will demonstrate how subtly the shapes can be simplified and developed to add another element to the sculpture (Fig 8.4). You will learn how rhythms can be created by repeating and opposing shapes (Fig 8.5), how the pressure of the body's high points pushes the material out smooth, adding variety and allowing the gathers and folds further away to

FIG 8.5   Chinese deity, possibly boxwood (Buxus sempervirens), date unknown. The folds follow the curves of the legs and stomach, and help them to be read as rounded forms. Notice the opposing rhythms of the folds diving between the thighs, and the repetition in the folds that lie on the ground. This shows that drapery can be treated in the same way the world over

FIG 8.6   Atalanta in cherry wood (Prunus avium), by Dick Onians

express tension (Fig 8.6). Certain lines indicate motion. The ancient Greeks used an ogival (flattened S) curve, such as I use in the demonstration piece here for the hair and the back line of the dress over the heel (see Fig 8.6). Other lines may simply draw the viewer's eye towards a gesture of the figure, to the face or to some object

FIG 8.4   Drapery study in Portland stone by Paul Maxwell. On the right: a maquette by the late Anna Johanssen, in which cloth soaked in emulsion (latex) paint is arranged to simulate drapery falling from the knee to break over a foot and onto the ground

FIG 8.7 *Two copies of a saint, possibly holding a heart, in seventeenth-century style, carved in lime by a duplicating machine. The right knee pushes out the folds so that they cascade in a series of angular forms. On the figure on the right the folds hang vertically and open out at the bottom rather like a linenfold pattern. The mould stains explain why they were never finished*

FIG 8.8 *In this view of Atalanta the left knee and the breasts are seen to push the drapery tight, with ridges running from them to indicate pressure and tension*

being held (Fig 8.7). Drapery may suggest lightness; it can also be used to support weak forms. What is particularly difficult is to get the same piece of drapery to give the same message to all viewpoints.

Planning the carving

The subject of the running woman was chosen to illustrate the draped figure partly because I like movement, and partly because it gives the opportunity to show how drapery can be exploited to emphasize movement. It combines

trailing folds with some parts of the body pressing against the material (Fig 8.8). It also adds support to all weak elements except the right forearm and the left foot.

To help with the composition of the drapery I first made a drawing of what would be the principal view (see Fig 8.14), then using this I made a maquette, starting with the nude figure. An armature of square aluminium wire was made, with one end rammed into a hole in a piece of softwood. Arms were made from a thinner piece of wire, fastened at the base of the neck with a wire tie. This joint was made rigid with car body filler, and the 'matchstick' woman was finally arranged (Fig 8.9) before building up the nude

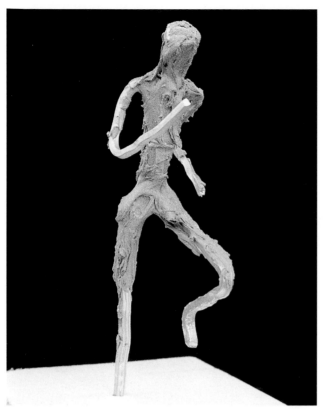

FIG 8.9 *The wire armature for Atalanta, partly covered with plastic metal (polyester resin with aluminium powder) commonly used for car body repairs*

FIG 8.10 *The nude figure developed enough for drapery to be laid over it. Note how the right leg slopes inwards to support the weight of the body*

figure with more of the metal filler. This was then rasped and cut to the desired shape (Fig 8.10). A piece of thin cloth was cut to the shape of a long, full skirt which would reach the ground at the back, and then dipped in white wood adhesive (PVA) diluted with water; emulsion (latex) paint also works. This was wrung out and arranged around the body to make the desired composition. As the adhesive began to stiffen, folds were opened out where they looked too thin, particularly those at the back and the flyaway fold outside the right leg. To simulate the drapery of the arms and torso, I used clay to represent a loose pullover. Clay was also used for the head and hair (Fig 8.11). This meant that I had to keep the maquette damp to prevent the clay's flaking off.

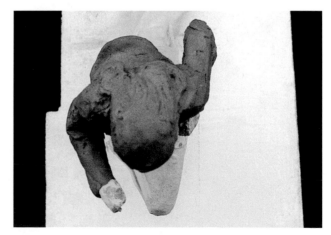

FIG 8.11 *This top view of the completed maquette shows that the arms, head and knee are arranged in a V to add to the effect of thrusting forward. The cloth is soaked in PVA adhesive and arranged from the waist down. Most of the folds occurred spontaneously, but the tail of the skirt was arranged and some folds opened out just before they set rigid. The pullover, head and hair are modelled in grey crank (clay)*

Of course the skirt is far too long for a real runner, but that is a consideration that never worried our forebears, who were more concerned with strength and artistic effect.

The wood chosen was cherry (*Prunus avium*), because it was close-grained, beautiful and available. The grain direction was chosen to give maximum strength. The right forearm would be weak however the grain ran through it. The dark bands in the wood show that this is reaction wood from a branch or a leaning tree, but the wood is dry and the carving is stout enough not to distort.

The carving procedure

The side profile was drawn onto the wood fairly loosely, working from the maquette (Fig 8.12). My way of working means that I do not make an exact copy of the maquette but, if you are satisfied that your model is complete and shows all you want the final sculpture to show, you may work very closely to it. Beware, however, lest the carving look more like clay than wood. I prefer to give myself room to develop forms as they emerge while I cut down to the final shape. It is difficult anyway to get the outline of a maquette accurately onto the wood. In this case I was able to lengthen the arms, which were rather short on the maquette.

You may cut the profile any way you like. The quickest and most efficient is with a bandsaw, which was used here. If you do this it is wise not to cut too closely to the outline. To save time, an Arbortech cutting disc can then be used to cut away the waste from in front of the head and other obvious waste areas (Fig 8.13). On a large sculpture you can rough out with a chainsaw.

FIG 8.12 The maquette seen from the side, with the pattern loosely drawn on the largest face of the block of wood. The grain direction was chosen so that its slope emphasized the lean of the figure, as well as contributing to the strength of the right arm

FIG 8.13 The outline bandsawn and some of the other surplus wood ground away with an Arbortech cutting disc mounted on an angle grinder. There are also a few chisel cuts

FIG 8.14 *An early stage showing the main shapes carved, next to the original drawing. Capturing the spirit of the piece is more important than making an exact copy. The original drawing is copied fairly closely in the maquette and in the subsequent carving, except that the drapery does not support the foot so well in the drawing*

FIG 8.15 *Another view of the duplicated saints of Fig 8.7; some of the folds have been filled in with clay to give an idea of how they might have been roughed out*

If you are copying from a model, you can draw the drapery folds onto the block at an early stage and cut around them to ensure that you always have enough wood reserved for them; indeed, the creases should be carved into the surface with a V-tool or a no. 11 gouge (Fig 8.14).

Fig 8.15 shows a detail of the two identical machine-carved figures of a saint in limewood (*Tilia* x *europaea*) which we have already seen in Fig 8.7. The clay filling some of the hollows demonstrates how it should be possible to block out the masses of drapery. It is a waste of time to mark in all the folds and keep recarving them, but it is necessary to mark some of the major lines in order to establish the proportions and movement. It is helpful to draw the undraped figure's outlines on the block both to fix the positions of the folds and, more importantly, to mark the parts of the body which the thinner parts of drapery will press against when the hollows between the folds are carved (Fig 8.16). In this design the tips of the

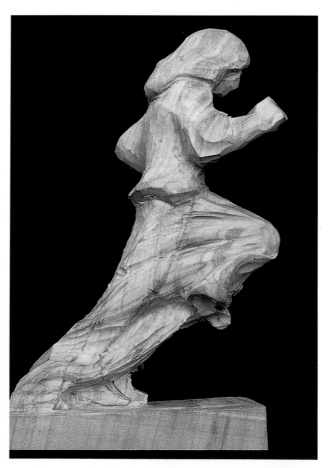

FIG 8.16 *The outline of the underlying left leg is drawn on to help fix the places where the drapery presses against it. Some main folds of the skirt have been established with a largish no. 11 gouge and V-chisel*

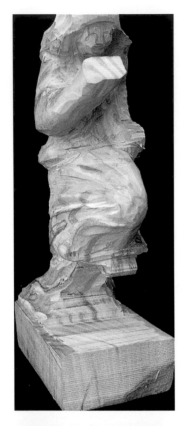

FIG 8.17 *The right knee is shaped early, as this is where the major folds of the skirt all start. Its shape is virtually what it would be if it were unclothed. The hands and face are still at an early stage*

FIG 8.18 *In the nearly finished carving the tension of the cloth on knee and chest is plain. Note how the ridges on the torso form a Z, which turns into a zigzag as the eye notices the folds of the skirt. The left hand is supported by contact with the thigh. The fingers and toes are not carved in detail, nor are the eyelids; they are not an essential part of the running effect*

elbows, the left knee and the breasts are pushing against the material. Parts of each shin and the thighs also show the body under the drapery. This is a useful way of keeping the proportions. It is important that the drapery does not invade the surface of the flesh; its thickness should always appear to rest on top of the skin (Fig 8.17). If a girdle or belt squeezes the waist, the skin and the cloth must behave reasonably and certainly not interrupt the bone structure.

The drapery around the legs is the most complex and so I decided to work on this first. One could copy every fold and twist but – while this may tell viewers that one has a good pair of eyes and painstaking technique – one might be putting down more than is needed to give a sense of exuberance and movement. If I had used a thicker material on the maquette, it probably would not have folded over its edges so much nor made such a confusing heap under the tail of the skirt. Judgement is used consciously and even unconsciously in selecting the significant details and omitting those which are distracting and unimportant. I prefer to simplify and develop shapes, but inexperienced carvers may feel safer with exact copying.

Folds and creases take various forms. Two cuts running side by side leave a slight ridge that may be all that is needed to convey tension and direction (Fig 8.18). Most often, drapery forms rounded ridges, frequently with deep folds between. The simplest form of these, as seen on early Greek sculpture of goddesses and on many effigies in churches, is a series of parallel folds, usually gathered at the waist and running to the ground or just above the foot. These corrugations may be quite deep. Sometimes the bottom edge

FIG 8.19 *The unfinished left side: the long ridges have been cut, but their ends are not yet shaped. The underside of the thigh has been marked with a shallow groove. A lump of wood has been kept for the folds on the inside of the elbow*

FIG 8.20 *The left side finished, immediately before the carving was sawn from its holding block. The ends of the ridges help to explain what the ridges are doing. The folds on the elbow are interlocking, as can be seen by comparison with the front view in Fig 8.18*

moves up and down with the end of each groove and ridge, like linenfold panelling. This helps the reading of the forms. Thin, rounded ridges may run from one high point to another, varying in thickness and depth from the ends towards the middle to suggest tension. On this carving you can see sharp ridges running diagonally from the breasts and on the back. From the left knee (Fig 8.19), narrow ridges open out as they move away. As on a linenfold panel, the edges of the material are shown turning up or down to add more life (Fig 8.20). Another common shape in drapery, much used particularly from the late Middle Ages, is the ridge which bifurcates, quite often creating an angle at the bifurcation. This is very common

on sleeves, and the angle can be seen if you look along the arm (see Fig 8.18). I have used this device on the elbows and the tops of the forearms (Figs 8.21 and 8.22), but mixed it with simple ridges to avoid monotony. It is also used on the right side of the saint (see Fig 8.15).

Two essentials to remember are that gravity is always at work even on a flowing garment, as in my runner, and that variety enlivens the carving. The same shapes repeated exactly may have a purpose as a pattern, but can look fussy or boring. As you look at the retreating runner, see how many ogival (shallow S-shaped) lines you can find (Fig 8.23; see also Fig 8.6).

FIG 8.21 *The inside angle of the right elbow at an early stage, with plenty of wood left for the folds. The drapery across the right leg is all established. Note the bifurcation of the big fold running from the left knee just above the flyaway flare*

FIG 8.22 *The inside angle of the elbow, with the ridges beginning to fan out. See Fig 8.6 for the finished result*

Tools and techniques

Planning the order of carving is important. Notice that the left foot has to be carved before finally shaping the drapery, and that to keep the piece strong the drapery is not undercut at the back until everything else is finished (Fig 8.24).

The more alike your folds are, the fewer chisels you need. For deep folds you need several deep gouges of different widths. No. 11 gouges are less likely to catch the grain and split the wood, but sometimes a no. 8 or no. 9 is useful as it can be rotated – the straight sides of a no. 11 prevent its

being used with a slicing movement when deep in the wood. V-tools can be used to mark out forms, but the bottoms of folds are seldom sharp unless the forms are deliberately stylized. You will find backbent gouges with a no. 3 or no. 5 sweep useful for the tops of the ridges in places where the base or vice might get in the way of a straight tool, and where the fold follows an inside curve, as in the flare to the right of the left knee. In the back view of the finished piece, the diagonal folds at the bottom also have inside curves on their upper edges. A straight gouge with an inside bevel may not be enough here. Likewise, various frontbent or spoon gouges, including a narrow no. 11 to fit

FIG 8.23 The finished carving from behind. See how many ogival lines there are in hair and drapery, and imagine the effect if they were straightened. It would probably work, but the sculpture would be stiffer and would lose some of its energy

FIG 8.24 The left foot has to be refined before the drapery around it can be finished. The undercutting of the right foot and the drapery behind it cannot be done until all strenuous carving is complete

the narrowest grooves, will save effort and produce a cleaner effect. Many folds will be diagonal to the grain, so, in finishing, additional cuts will be needed to stroke the fibres with the grain on each side. There are times when small rotary cutters and burrs will work well, but you will need to use chisels to produce a clean, crisp finish.

Drapery offers great opportunities for exploring shapes and enhancing designs, but it will never be convincing unless the form underneath it is in the right proportion and is kept in mind at all times.

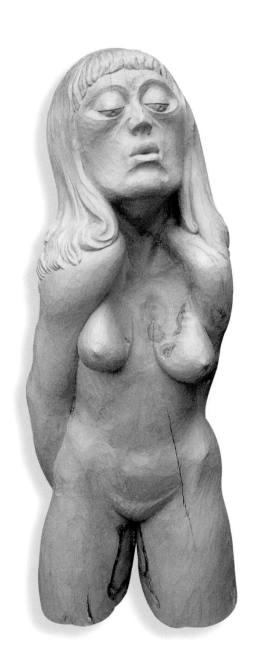

Chapter

STYLIZING THE FIGURE

O nce you have learned how the figure is shaped in nature, you are in a good position to experiment with simplifying it, developing it so that it expresses more closely the feelings that you have about it, without being tied to literal accuracy. For many artists the essence of art is to present ideas as economically as possible (Fig 9.1). If you portray every aspect of the figure, the viewer cannot identify your main interest in making it. Indeed, the surface detail may so dominate that the underlying forms are hidden – which may be a valid purpose, but is hardly sculpture. This chapter considers the reasons for stylizing the figure, what to look out for, and various approaches to designing such a figure.

Stylization and how we see

Stylization of any plant, animal or human figure is not necessarily deliberate. The culture in which one lives may have conditioned one to see these forms in a simplified way, and even taught how to exploit them as patterns as a matter of course (Fig 9.2). Conversely, because a child has not been conditioned, its drawings pick out what is essential. Everything is simplified: often the head and body are round, arms and legs are sticks, eyes

FIG 9.1 *Torso in English walnut (Juglans regia) by Tina Shafran. The whole is very carefully planned and understated; it is still unfinished, as she is determined to get it exactly right. The back of the sculpture is hollowed*

In earlier times, accurate representational sculptors such as Michelangelo and Bernini were exciting because they were themselves excited by their striving for accuracy. They were improving on what had gone before. In the West we have been conditioned by centuries of the classical tradition to see the world very literally. Since the mid-nineteenth century with the advent of the camera and, more recently, with advanced mould-making techniques, artists have been trying to break away from what was becoming a stale tradition. But the legacy still holds sway in some quarters, where there is what many regard as an excessive concentration on actual detail. Every wrinkle, every hair, every muscle has to be reproduced. Too often our eye dwells on the surface detail and may not even notice slipshod modelling of the underlying forms. Even if the modelling is accurate, we may find the whole effect a sterile demonstration of technique. We may gasp at the sculptor's co-ordination of hand and eye, but we learn nothing about the subject that looking at the real thing does not teach us.

FIG 9.2 African carving (wood unknown), c.1975, showing exaggerated features and intuitive use of rhythm

and other facial features are exaggeratedly either large or small. The child concentrates on those parts that are important to it. Perhaps the words that children use limit their ability to see. The finer details of anatomy are not normally learnt until later. Similarly, the drawings of early man usually show matchstick figures and animals; it is sufficient that the symbols are recognizable. However, even in the work of artists whom we, in our sophisticated way, call 'primitive', we find a deliberate or unconscious development of shapes to make elegant or pleasing patterns.

The best representational artists give us only the illusion that they have put in every detail and that the modelling is strictly accurate, whereas in reality they have exaggerated the modelling to provide strong shadows so that the whole can be read from afar. The details, too, are not so thorough as we are made to believe. Most people see what they expect to see, and a good sculptor takes advantage of this fact – although he does not use it cynically or through incompetence to disguise poor work, as I am afraid some others do. These latter may indeed benefit from the fact that our imaginations not only complete an imperfect image or a badly made sculpture, but even endue it with a perfection which the actual object could never otherwise have.

FIG 9.3 *Female figure in English walnut by Eva Andrusier. The main concern of the carver was to give the figure lift and movement while keeping the forms compact. This design would be feasible in stone*

FIG 9.4 *Matchstick figure in the form of a letter P, in cedar of Lebanon (Cedrus libani), by Dick Onians. Note how the angular lines stress the shapes*

Many figure sculptors have moved even further, to make more impressionistic or expressive forms (Fig 9.3). They single out what appears significant in the chosen pose, not because they cannot make an accurate representation but because they do not wish to be distracted by what in that instance seems irrelevant (Fig 9.4). (Perhaps this is not quite true today, when life study is apparently neglected in our art schools; even when life drawing is taught, it is encouraged to be what is called 'gestural' – that is, more impressionistic than closely observed.)

Stylization in western art now is nearly always deliberate. Beginners in carving who have little or no experience of studying the human figure may stylize because they know that there is little chance of their doing an accurate representation (Fig 9.5). However, if their stylization does succeed it is only because they have an innate sense of design in three dimensions, or have studied design. Too often we cannot rise above the conditioning of our tradition and the result falls between two stools, being neither accurate representation nor effective stylization. People who have never seen art in the classical tradition have a better chance of success;

FIG 9.5 Adam *in lime (Tilia x europaea) by Dick Onians, before he had been to life drawing classes. Note the wrong proportions, 'rubber' arm and exaggerated fingers and eye sockets. They do not necessarily make it a bad sculpture but they do show inexperience*

Fig 9.6 Family *in spalted field maple (Acer campestre) by Dick Onians. This is a maquette for a large public wood sculpture, hence its rough state. The forms are recognizable, but simple and strong*

their ignorance may unconsciously lead to attractive stylization. The way most likely to guarantee success is to have a thorough knowledge of the human figure. Then the carver knows what he or she is taking liberties with.

Stylization in public sculpture

Today there seems to be a growing interest in having large wood sculptures in public places. This may be because wood is cheaper and more available than stone. Also, the public is readier to accept that works of art do not have to be made to last for centuries. Perhaps, too, the public bodies commissioning such work realize that for the usually small sums of money they are prepared to spend they cannot expect the durability of stone or metal. Pieces of wood sculpture which are exposed to the weather as well as the physical attentions of passers-by need to be robust, so inevitably the forms must be simplified. Stone and metal sculptures, of course, must also be designed to endure. The stylized human figure lends itself to this, and is acceptable where more abstract work would encounter intransigent prejudice (Fig 9.6).

Approaches to stylizing the figure

One fruitful approach to stylization is to make a sculpture that is accurate or only slightly simplified, and then see how those shapes that seem to contain the essence of the figure or the pose could be developed while simplifying or omitting what seems irrelevant. You may want to elongate the figure, or make it more squat. You may emphasize the roundness of forms, or you may try breaking the whole into rectangles or other angular geometrical solids; or you may simply develop lines and masses into rhythms that express some strong personal feeling about the pose (Figs 9.7–9.9). What you will notice is that the carving takes on some of the properties of a caricature or a diagram. An exciting procedure is to do a series of carvings, progressively simplifying the forms until you think that you have captured the very essence (Figs 9.10–9.12). You may end with something that is completely abstract and that would be unrecognizable to anyone who had not seen the sequence. With care, every carving will be a good piece with its own appeal. This is a recipe that any carver starting from an animal, plant or other real object can profitably follow.

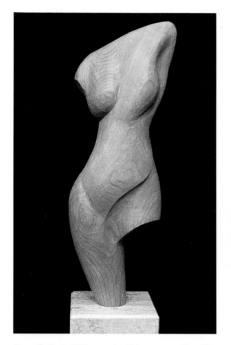 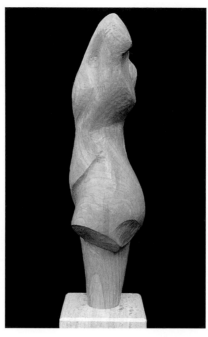 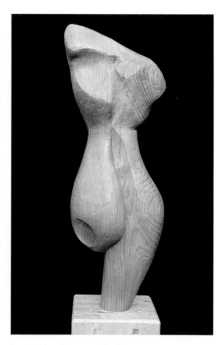

FIGS 9.7–9.9 *Torso in false camellia (Stewartia pseudocamellia) by Sally Rose: front, side and back views. Sally has used the natural forms as a basis for an exciting design. The eye is easily carried around as the forms are consistent all over the figure*

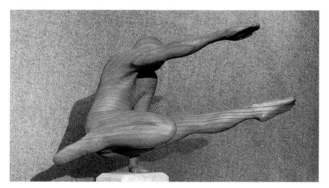

FIG 9.10 Hurdler *in Indian bean (Catalpa bignonioides) by Dick Onians. The details of fingers, toes and face have been omitted but the muscles are more or less accurate. The sculpture is mounted on stone with a screw which travels up through the base and through the lower arm up to the elbow, where the short grain of the arm is supported by the wood of the thigh*

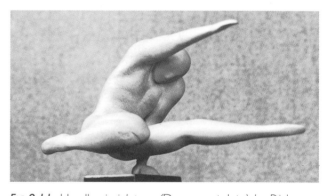

FIG 9.11 Hurdler *in jelutong (Dyera costulata) by Dick Onians. The shapes of feet, hands and head have been simplified still further*

FIG 9.12 Hurdler *in recycled Cuban mahogany (Swietenia mahogani) by Dick Onians. The composition has been abstracted so that only the movement is retained. Both this and the jelutong version are mounted in the same way as the catalpa one*

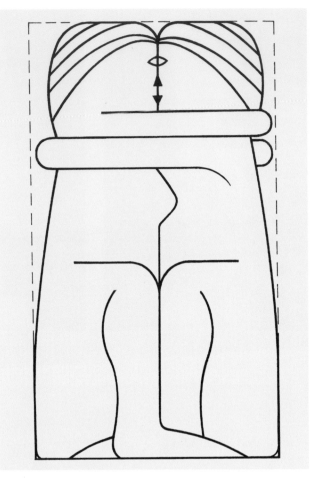

FIG 9.13 *Face emerging from a burred log of mulberry (Morus nigra), by Kathleen Chapman. Minimal wood has been removed*

FIG 9.14 *Drawing inspired by a sculpture by Constantin Brancusi in his 'Kiss' series of stone carvings. The message is clear enough without any more shaping. This looks a very economical form of expression, but has been carefully planned. The modelling is very shallow*

Another approach is to fit the shapes of the human body to the shape of the piece of wood by removing as little of the material as possible (Fig 9.13). This understatement is very effective and can have the magic of 'primitive' work, which is powerful because it appears to express the heart of its message with minimum effort. In fact, what is more likely is that the primitive maker was restricted by having to work in a difficult material with simple tools, and having conveyed his idea he did not feel the need to elaborate on it. To achieve the same feeling with the sophisticated equipment at our disposal is very difficult. However, the chainsaw and angle grinder, having large cutting edges, lend themselves to simplification. Since the beginning of the twentieth century, when artists such as Picasso and Epstein became excited by African and other sculpture previously ignored or derided as barbaric, various artists have successfully become 'primitive' (Fig 9.14). It is worth noticing that even when their forms retain a strong memory of the original square block, these sculptures can be read clearly in the round.

A particularly fertile source for stylization is the mask (Figs 9.15–9.21). Because masks have commonly been used in theatrical performances and religious rites, they have had to be able to make their point when seen from a distance: they therefore need to be exaggerated or simplified. As eyes and mouth are the most obviously expressive parts of the head, they are invariably the most emphasized. They can be made into strong forms with a definite pattern, or they can be understated but still become noticeable because all other features have been effaced. A welter of fine details would obscure the effect and be hard to read from a distance.

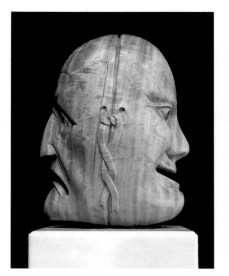

FIGS 9.15–9.17 Combined masks of Tragedy and Comedy in West Indian satinwood (Fagara flava) by Dick Onians: side view showing how the masks are linked. This is fairly naturalistic, but even here the eyes and mouth are exaggerated

FIGS 9.18 AND 9.19 Back-to-back masks of Tragedy and Comedy in sweet chestnut (Castanea sativa) by Dick Onians. In this more stylized carving, note how the eyebrows and lines of the face have been made to form patterns. The two masks are again linked with ribbons

FIG 9.20 *Tragi-comedy in plane* (Platanus *sp.) by Dick Onians, showing a further stylization verging on the abstract. The two masks flow one into the other*

FIG 9.21 *Tragedy side of another combined head in sweet chestnut* (Castanea sativa), *following the same sort of development as the previous one*

In a still figure it is probable that the features of the face, hands and feet will be indicated, even if only scratched on the surface; indeed, the features may be the main element of the stylization (Fig 9.22). But when the intention is to capture a moving pose, the facial details, fingers and toes, navel and genitals can be omitted (Fig 9.23). A draped figure already offers opportunities for most of these to be lost (see Fig 8.8 on page 120). However, some indication of details may be needed to remove ambiguity. Sometimes, too, an otherwise blank shape may need some detail added to maintain interest. For the same reason a line may be cut into long, flowing drapery, with the added advantage that it can be used to carry the viewer's eyes from one part of the composition to another, and add some sort of rigidity without which the form may look floppy.

Respecting the limitations of the material

The techniques used in carving the stylized human figure are exactly the same as those needed for a representational one. However, if a matchstick-like figure is intended, it may be more necessary than with a representational figure to use the gentler pressure of a riffler, rather than a chisel.

Wood allows a wider variety of poses than stone, but its limits must always be respected. A compact composition (see Fig 9.3) or one elongated along the grain is the most suitable. Any design that involves short grain running through load-bearing parts – usually arms or legs – invites trouble. As stylization often involves turning a figure into a matchstick person, this danger is common (Fig 9.24). Wood with branches may be used to avoid this, but carries its own problems because of

FIG 9.22 Holly Woman *in holly (Ilex aquifolium) by Dick Onians. Shapes are exaggerated; note particularly the stylization of the face. This is fairly naturalistic, but even here the eyes and mouth are exaggerated and made into a deliberate pattern. The carving of the body has been affected by included bark and other problems with the wood*

FIG 9.23 Odalisque *in almond (Prunus dulcis) by Dick Onians. The spindly forms are supported where they are short-grained. The left arm is straight along the grain for strength*

FIG 9.24 Gymnasts *in lime by Sylvia Worthington. This lively piece contains so much short grain that it was essential to break it so it could be reinforced with dowels*

complicated changes of grain. You may not like adding pieces of wood with a different grain direction, as the joint is usually distracting. However, if it suits you, you can disguise this by painting (as was frequently done historically) or by careful staining. A practical solution for thin, short-grained elements is to break the piece carefully and insert a dowel; or, in the case of a thin, short-grained leg or arm that touches the ground, drill up through the base and as far as possible through the weak part and insert a dowel or screw (see Figs 9.10–9.12). Both methods demand great care and skill. It should also be remembered that a dowel,

particularly a metal one, might smash the wood around it if the carving is later damaged. I prefer to use bamboo, as it will either bend or snap without harming the surrounding wood. Bamboo kebab sticks make excellent small dowels.

When designing a stylized figure, it is much more rewarding to use your own ideas. Quite apart from the risk of prosecution if you pass off as your own something which is copied from or recognizably inspired by someone else's work, there is never the same satisfaction as there is in knowing that it is yours from start to finish.

THE FIGURE IN RELIEF

One of the commonest subjects for woodcarvers is the scene in relief consisting either of a whole or partial human figure, or of a scene containing at least one person. This is not strange, as wood is easily bought in boards and relief is the closest the woodcarver gets to pictures in two dimensions. Yet, because it is fraught with risks for the inexperienced, it has been kept until the final chapter of this book.

One advantage of relief carving is that you can set your subjects in a context such as a building or a landscape, which enables you to tell a story fairly easily (Fig 10.1). The other advantage is that because the background is able to give support, you can arrange your subjects in poses that would be very difficult to achieve in the round in a material like wood or stone which would not sustain delicate or short-grained forms.

Art and the nature of seeing

When sculptors describe themselves as artists the usual response in Britain is: 'What do you paint?' This betrays a cultural and educational background that has given little prominence to three-dimensional work. This may change as awareness of sculpture grows; nevertheless, the major reason why

FIG 10.1 *This panel illustrates the poem 'Mowing' by Robert Frost, beginning: 'There was never a sound beside the wood but one, | And that was my long scythe whispering to the ground.' The board is lime (Tilia x europaea) with the grain running horizontally. The grain could have been vertical, but this would not have suited the sky so well. A pale, lightly figured wood allows shadows to be seen easily. Lime, which is harder than its American relation, basswood (Tilia americana), takes carving against the grain, which also makes it suitable for working in awkward spots; but a harder, close-grained wood that does not splinter would also work well. The tricks of perspective, foreshortening and tilting the hills and sky forward all contribute to the illusion of depth. The big tree on the left is actually level with the front plane of the wood*

we prefer making pictures lies in the way we see. Our brains receive from our eyes a flat picture of the world, and we have learnt that this has depth only because we can move around and touch things. This not only explains why relief carving is a popular subject, but also why it is about the most difficult to do. Few people naturally have a three-dimensional grasp of the visual world, and some do not understand perspective. To carve successful relief scenes in our Western idiom you need both abilities, which can be learnt.

The evolution of relief

Relief pictures probably originated from the simple act of scratching a drawing on bone, wood, stone or clay. Since the invention of the V-chisel, the simplest form of relief in wood has been to use it to cut all the lines of the drawing onto the wood (Fig 10.2). This can be developed, first by varying the thicknesses of the lines and the angles of the cuts so that they create shadow or reflect light, and then by subtly modelling the

Fig 10.2 The use of a V-tool to perpetuate the drawing. This simple cutting of the lines must have been a precursor to creating true relief in early art

surfaces that the lines enclose. This is the lowest relief. The ancient Egyptians were so expert at this that with the right lighting they could make such carvings appear to have considerable depth. A less sophisticated (but more strenuous) development is to relieve the object from its background by removing surrounding material to produce a raised silhouette (Fig 10.3). This stage can be taken further by the modelling of the surface, to produce the form of relief most familiar to us.

The advantage of relief over simply scratching a drawing is that light and shade make it appear to stand out, which makes the design more readable from afar. Between the shallow incised outline and the sculpture which is carved virtually completely in the round against a background, there is a range of relief styles. There are three main categories: high, medium and low (*bas* in French) relief. The incised relief mentioned above is an extreme form of low relief. Sometimes two forms, or all three, are used in the same picture.

FIG 10.3 An ancient Kashmiri suttee memorial stone (by courtesy of Dr C. K. Atal). The widow is on the funeral pyre while her dead husband's ghost sits on his horse awaiting her arrival. The figures are raised above the background. The horse and rider are only slightly rounded, while the remaining detail is largely superficial

I have illustrated them with a sampler in mulberry (*Morus* sp.) (Figs 10.4 and 10.5) and others in Quebec yellow pine (*Pinus strobus*) (Figs 10.6 and 10.7). I have included incised relief with the low relief example in mulberry as well as in the yellow pine sampler, and in a carving illustrating themes from a poem by William Wordsworth (see Fig 10.12).

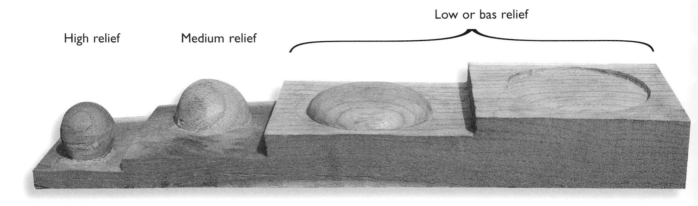

FIG 10.4 *A simplified representation of the three types of relief. High relief (left) is virtually in the round and may even be partially detached from the background. In medium relief, half the subject is lost in the background; the visible part is probably not foreshortened. In bas-relief there is much foreshortening. The incised relief on the far right tends to be shallow, but uses the shadows created by both sides of the incision. In this example some parts of the wood are darker than the rest, having been carved a month earlier*

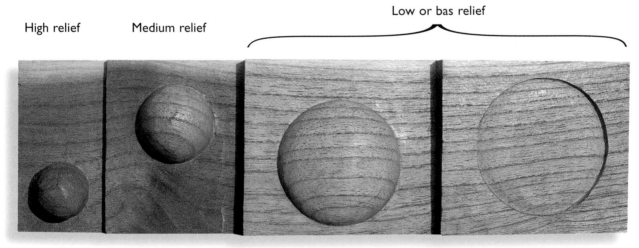

FIG 10.5 *The shadows cast by the different types of relief show their relative effectiveness.*

FIG 10.6 *These examples show how incised relief can be given different effects by varying the slope of the outside of the V-cut. The line across the circle has necessitated a slight depression on each side which the eye barely notices. The centre of the other circle is slightly hollowed too, to show how the eye can be deceived into reading a hollow as a bump*

142

FIG 10.7 Notice how the shape of the uninterrupted circle appears more round when the lighting is reversed. In Fig.10.6 the top right-hand side is set down vertically from the ground. This casts a shadow onto the circle. With the lighting reversed, the gentler slope of the opposite side means that its shadow does not impinge on the disc

Perspective and foreshortening

You may deliberately flout the rules of perspective and concentrate on the symbolic aspects of your subject matter if you are working in a 'primitive' vein or have a naturally eccentric way of seeing the world (Fig.10.8). However, most carvers when they begin relief try to make a photographic representation because that is what they are accustomed to seeing; but without a good understanding of perspective and foreshortening they often create an uncomfortable combination of primitive vision with Western sophistication.

If you copy a photograph or drawing you will seldom find that it was made with the eye at ground level, so on a human figure, for example, the further foot appears higher up the picture. It will also appear smaller than the nearer one. 'Perspective' is the name for the way objects and parts of objects move up and down the picture plane depending on the position of the viewer, and for the way in which objects appear smaller the further away they are. Parallel lines seem to converge and diminish to a vanishing point. Railway sleepers (railroad ties), telegraph poles, railings, trees in avenues and architectural forms appear not only to shrink but also to become

FIG 10.8 The Fall of Jericho carved in elm (Ulmus procera) by Leslie Lonsdale-Cooper. This is inspired by the Romanesque style, where the story was of greater importance than literal representation. The city and the temple are shown in different perspectives, and Joshua is bigger than the priests because he is more important to the story

closer together with distance. We can use such features to help with the interpretation of the relief. It is possible to study perspective scientifically, like technical drawing, but you can also learn it by careful observation and practice.

If you place a rectangular object (such as a matchbox) at eye level so that you see its whole width, and then turn it slightly, the width of that side appears to shrink. This is foreshortening in the two-dimensional plane. There may be little perspective visible in so short an object, but in a longer one the further end is noticeably less high.

'Foreshortening' also describes the compression into, say, ¾in (19mm) of a subject that in the round would occupy many times that distance. Low and medium reliefs involve more or less foreshortening in this sense of the term. If a figure is compressed in depth but still occupies its usual outlines in the other two dimensions, some foreshortening occurs. It will appear quite out of proportion when seen edgeways (see, for example, Figs 10.19 and 10.34).

Representing perspective and foreshortening in relief

If you lie with your eye at ground level, people and other upright elements in the scene, such as trees, are usually at right angles to the ground, which is visible only as a single line. You can show that some of these things are further away than others by making them diminish with distance and carving them successively deeper into the wood.

If, however, the ground is below eye level – as it normally is when you stand or sit – it will appear to rise before you. To indicate depth you will need to make a noticeable change of angle between the ground and the objects upon it. If the ground stays parallel with the back of the board you are carving it from, a standing person in the scene will have to tilt forward so as to look perpendicular to the ground plane. However, as the wood is too thin to make them actually perpendicular, you will have to use a flatter angle. Too sharp an angle may also create the impression that you are looking down on the scene from directly above. Alternatively you may slope the ground away from the bottom edge of your picture up to the horizon. If this is far away, there is a danger of carving through the wood or making the angle of the ground so shallow that it is hard to see the contrast between the ground and the things standing on it. This contrast becomes less important with distance. You will often find that as the distance in the real world increases, so the slope on the panel diminishes, until distant parts of the view actually curve forwards again. The important thing to remember is that if there is an angle in the real scene there must be one in your relief, even if it is only where the feet meet the ground. One way to work out how to apply perspective and foreshortening is to make preparatory studies in clay.

Illusion

Relief, like drawing on paper, is a matter of illusion. Representational art is the business of representing things with what they are not. In art generally we are used to symbols and conventional treatments. But, as my teacher, the late William Wheeler, put it more bluntly, 'With relief you often have to tell lies in order to tell the truth.' You may also say that if a sculpture looks right it *is* right. It is therefore quite acceptable to make the top edges of hills project from the background

FIG 10.9 *The* Mowing *panel, showing how the distant hills and the sky are tilted forwards*

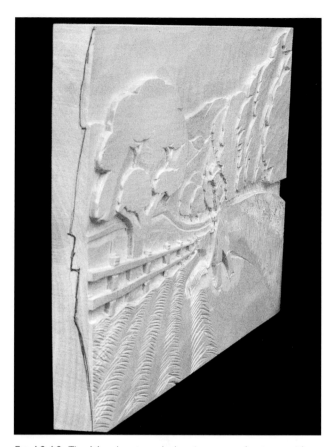

FIG 10.10 *The* Mowing *panel, showing an early stage with the anticipated depths drawn on the end*

(Fig 10.9). It is possible to have distant objects in the same plane as things in the foreground. Some sculptors insist on keeping some part of everything (except perhaps sky) at the level of the front of the panel. It is even possible to carve something to look convex by hollowing all or part of its surface so it holds the light appropriately in its final situation (see Figs 10.6 and 10.7).

Three approaches to relief carving

To illustrate how the problems of relief can be solved, I present three panels: two where the figures are set in landscape, and one which is a portrait against a flat background. The landscape dominates the panel with the mower, and shows

how perspective can be enhanced by foreshortening and by playing tricks with distance. I carefully devised the drawing, mentally planning how the depths would be interpreted, as you can see from the end view in the early stages of carving (Fig 10.10). The carving was begun by V-cutting the drawing just to demonstrate the effectiveness of this technique (see Fig 10.2), but this is a slow way to start if you are intending to carve in depth.

The preparation for the carvings of the scenes from Wordsworth and my mother's portrait took the form of drawings followed by maquettes made with grey crank, a heavily grogged clay. With a coarse, gritty clay like this one has to keep the forms simple and strong, thus avoiding the trap of concentrating on superficial detail at the expense of readable sculpture. Clay is better than modelling materials such as Plasticine or one of the modern reinforced clays, in that it cuts easily without distortion. Clay modelling mainly involves building up, but one is also able to carve parts away and rearrange them (Fig 10.11). It is far better to make one's mistakes in such an easily corrected medium. Because one has to leave some details to the carving stage, there is not too much chance of the carving's becoming a sterile copy. The purpose of any preparatory work is to reduce the amount of thinking which has to be done during the actual carving. This reduces hesitation

and makes for livelier, more confident and faster carving. With any unfamiliar subject, but especially with the foreshortening involved in relief work, a maquette is essential.

The Wordsworth panel (Fig 10.12) was devised to show three different depths of relief in the figures, so the landscape merely provides a setting to link them. Here, because it was my own design, once the clay interpretation was adjusted to my satisfaction I worked out where each block would fit into the wood but did not draw the pattern on at first (Fig 10.13); this is not necessary if the picture is firmly in your head as well as in your clay maquette. This

FIG 10.11 The clay sketch for the panel illustrating elements in the poem by Wordsworth on 'Intimations of Immortality Based on Recollections of Early Childhood'

FIG 10.12 On the finished panel, from the left, I illustrate the lines: 'And see the Children sport upon the shore, | And hear the mighty waters rolling evermore.' This is followed by: 'Shout round me, let me hear thy shouts, thou happy Shepherd-boy!' Next: 'Shades of the prison-house begin to close | Upon the growing Boy.' The Boy gazes across a valley at '. . . a Tree, of many, one, | A single Field which I have looked upon'. Finally, the adult Wordsworth contemplates a flower, possibly a pansy, and declares that 'To me the meanest flower that blows can give | Thoughts that do often lie too deep for tears.' The children on the shore, being a distant memory of an existence before this life, are portrayed in incised relief

method is worth trying, but only if you have a strong mental image of the intended result. Subsequently the outline is drawn on, and the carving follows the usual pattern (Figs 10.14–10.18). I have not

FIG 10.13 *Areas where there will be raised parts are isolated quickly. The outline of the cliff top is already set in fairly freely. The cross marks the middle of the panel as a reminder not to divide the design into halves*

FIG 10.14 *The principal elements have been drawn on and more or less closely set in. There are planes cut across the chests of the shepherd-boy and the growing boy, and on the wall of the prison-house. The adult has been crudely outlined*

FIG 10.15 *The planes of the figure of the adult are indicated before the outline is closely cut in*

FIG 10.16 *The planes are further developed and the outline is cut closer to the finished shape*

FIG 10.17 *The head projects more than the rest, so it is finished first*

FIG 10.18 *When he is finished, we seem to be looking down at him and the flower. We see his feet and forearms almost in plan view. His head and face are not foreshortened, but as we go down the figure his upper arms, torso and legs below the knees become increasingly foreshortened. The wild pansy or heartsease flower is in the transitional area between the man's perspective and that of the foreground, but we still look down on its leaves*

restricted myself by cutting vertically against the outline immediately. You can see how the foreshortening of the figure on the right representing the adult Wordsworth gradually evolved, and how when viewed from the side the figure appears distorted (Fig 10.19). At the left is the lowest relief. The outlines here were stabbed with gouges that fitted the shapes (Fig 10.20) or chased with a V-tool, and the surface gently modelled to create highlights and shadows (Fig 10. 21).

A head in relief is far more difficult than a scene, particularly if you aim to get a good likeness. To do my mother's head I took photographs and made drawings of many views to learn the shapes (Fig 10.22). As with the general anatomy, our

FIG 10.19 *From the side the adult looks deformed. Just past the bushes, you can see how the bent leg of the youth has been curved around the straight one so that the foot can rest against the wall. This deception is not noticeable from the front*

FIG 10.20 *The children on the shore have been drawn, the waves have been cut with a V-tool, and the cutting of the children's outlines has been started by stabbing down with a small shallow gouge*

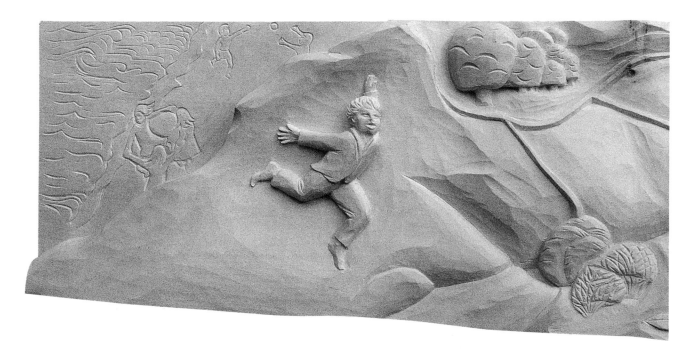

FIG 10.21 *The surfaces of the children have been modelled to catch the light and give them depth*

FIG 10.22 *Drawings of the head of Rosalind Onians, from photographs. The profile on the right has little modelling of the surface. More modelling has been drawn onto the jaw on the far left. The shadows elsewhere are only slightly helpful; they show changes of direction of the surface but do not describe them. The more views of the head are drawn, the better the chosen view will be understood*

knowledge even of the faces of those dearest to us is inadequate without careful study, preferably with the aid of drawings. Because it is the most difficult subject, I give a full description of the carving of the head (pages 154–7).

A scene can be comparatively easily analysed as a series of planes and curved surfaces, but the transitions from one part of a head to another are subtle. I refer to the head, rather than the face, because the face accounts for only about a third of the distance between the tip of the nose and the back of the head. Nor does the face end in a hard line, like a mask. Even a face seen directly from the front does not make up the total silhouette as, apart from the obvious hair and ears, the skull continues to rise behind the hairline and gets broader behind the ears. Probably because the words we use for

them tend to make us think of the parts of the head as separate items, many inexperienced sculptors carve them as if they were separate. The result is that in many carvings eyes are given hard outlines, noses do not flow off the cheeks, and corners of mouths become sharp and goblin-like. This applies as much to relief as to carving in the round. Problems of foreshortening compound the difficulty.

An excellent lesson in shallow relief is to be seen in heads on coins (Fig 10.23). The monarch's head on British coins shows some eye detail and modelling of the cheek in front of the eye, the nostril, the lips, the ear, the back of the jaw and the hair. There is a slight curve over the cheek and from the temple to where the forehead meets the background. The skull, hair and neck are as carefully modelled as the face.

Fig 10.23 Heads of George VI and Elizabeth II, showing how sophisticated shallow relief can be. These are far more than silhouettes

More difficult than either the full face or the side profile is a partial front and side view, which is how I have chosen to carve my mother. Here there is no clear and quickly recognizable profile, nor is there symmetry. Also, a far greater depth of the head is visible.

In the head of D. H. Lawrence carved by William Wheeler (Figs 10.24 and 10.25), the further eye and cheek are virtually at the surface, level with the nearer side. This means the features, particularly the subtleties of cheeks and forehead, have to be given shallow treatment. By making the tops of the hollows under the cheekbone, under the cheek and above the mouth turn proportionately faster than in nature, a strong shadow is created. If the modelling is too subtle it will not show except with strong side lighting.

FIG 10.24 *Head of D. H. Lawrence carved in lime by William Wheeler as a master for a bronze cast. Note the heavy shadows, effective in wood and essential to show on bronze. The hair is carved freely with a mixture of highlights and shadows*

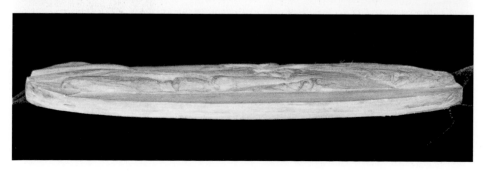

FIG 10.25 *Edge view of the face of D. H. Lawrence, showing the shallowness of relief. The height of the left side of the face is virtually at the front of the wood*

Working from a photograph

A method which you can use, and which I used here, is to project a slide photograph onto paper and use that for your outline; but additional studies, such as drawings, will be needed to help with the reading of the depths of the forms. An enlarged photocopy of a photographic print can also be used. The distortion produced by the camera is acceptable on subjects of this size, but needs to be compensated for with anything bigger. My drawings lack the sculptural form I would

normally put into a portrait, but the outlines do guarantee that the features will have the actual relationship to each other that they have in two dimensions. This certainly helps with setting down the outline.

To prepare for carving, I flattened a bed of clay on a board (protected by polythene to prevent the wet clay from affecting it) and pricked the outlines onto it through a drawing. Bearing in mind the thickness of the wood to be used, I first built up clay to the highest points (Fig 10.26),

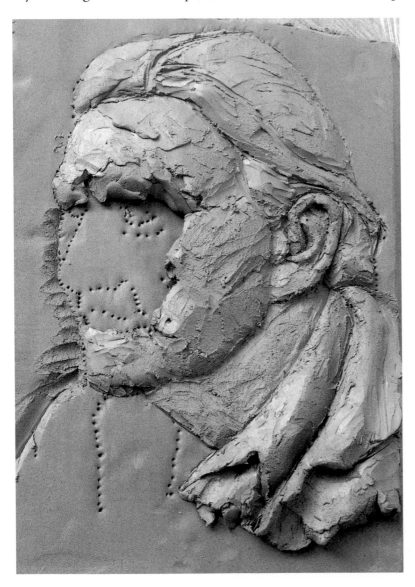

FIG 10.26 After the outline of Rosalind Onians' head has been pricked onto a slab of clay, further clay is built up on the outline, establishing the main high points: brow, cheek and near collar

then added the rest accordingly, modelling the foreshortened forms as the thickness of the material allowed (Fig 10.27). This method creates a better sense of depth than carving the shape directly into a thick layer of clay. As the wet clay had affected the paper of the original drawing, I used a photocopy over carbon paper to transfer the outline to a limewood board measuring 11¼ x 8¾ x 1½in (286 x 222 x 38mm). I then marked a line around the sides of the wood at the level intended for the ground.

One question that immediately arises once the ground has been set down is how the forms inside the outline can be kept in their proper positions as the surface of the head is carved away. One way is to glue your drawing onto a piece of thin card and, with a needle, prick through the drawing into the wood. This ensures that the original drawing on the surface of the wood is not permanently lost. Obviously you will produce a more lively and spontaneous carving if you eschew such a rigid approach and draw the details freehand.

FIG 10.27 *The finished clay maquette*

FIG 10.28 *The ground in the process of being lowered. As the further shoulder is so low, it is worth carving down away from the collar towards the edge of the wood. Elsewhere, vertical cuts have been made just outside the outline, followed by cuts across the grain towards the head*

FIG 10.29 *The outline of the head and shoulders has now been set down to meet the background at a right angle. The final depth has been reached, so the full depth of wood to be modelled is visible. If the chisel slips and marks the background, a judicious paring of the surface should correct it without making any noticeable difference*

Carving the head

I cut the ground away downwards from the outline with a 1¼in (32mm) no. 8 gouge, and used a ½in (12mm) no. 11 to level the ground across the grain towards the outline (Fig 10.28). Various gouges that fitted the shapes were used to set down the outline to the ground level. The ground was then smoothed to its final surface with large Swiss no. 2 and no. 3 gouges (Fig 10.29).

It is tempting, where you have a mark on the surface of the wood, to cut vertically in order to transmit the shape to a lower level. This is risky. It

is safer to cut an internal form with a veiner or a V-tool, since the bottom of the cut is less likely to go too deep. As the sides of the cut also slope, the exact final position of a line can be adjusted according to the judgement of the carver. You must remember that what looks right on a flat piece of paper can be wrong when the surface area of the wood is increased by the modelling, and when shadows are created.

I used a big V-chisel and the no. 11 to run around the jaw and hair lines and set down the nose profile and lip division, remembering to stop well before reaching the further cheek (Fig 10.30).

FIG 10.30 *The fierce lighting shows the front-facing parts of the brow, nose and upper lip sloped towards the ground and the profile of the nose cut in. The hair, jaw and throat lines have been cut in with a large V-chisel. The slope of the near cheek down to the hair and the back of the jaw has been begun*

Possible errors

Principal errors in head carving are to carve too heavily under the eyebrows, not to make the cheek sweep up onto the nose, and to miss the hollow that runs diagonally up across the cheek into the hollow between the inside corner of the eye and the nose. There is also a hollow under the cheekbone which effectively starts from the last-mentioned diagonal and fades out in the direction of the upper rim of the ear. The narrowness of the temple is often missed. The zygomatic arch – the part of the cheekbone that runs horizontally back to the ear – is usually far more prominent than the temple.

FIG 10.31 *Modelling of the hair and forehead, cheek and near eyeball has begun, with cuts with a no. 11 gouge. By cutting across the grain one is very conscious of the undulations of the forms, and by keeping the corners of the gouge out of the wood one avoids nasty surprises that an irregular grain might spring. The sharp cut under the eyebrow is done with a veiner, and has left room for the rounded area above*

As with a landscape, relative planes are represented with flattened angles. If you draw a line from top to bottom of the head which follows the watershed between the parts facing forwards and those facing sideways, you may carve around the forms with a deep gouge in each direction. As you carve downwards across the cheek, remember to raise the chisel as it meets the nose. The side of the nose is facing in almost the same direction as the near side of the head (Figs 10.31 and 10.32).

FIG 10.32 The modelling is almost complete except for the ear, the further eye and cheek, and the collars of blouse and cardigan. Note the light on top of the cheekbone and the V-shaped hollow below it. Details of eyelids, nostril and mouth also remain to be done

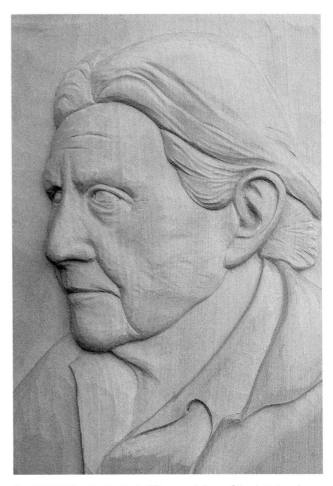

FIG 10.33 The finished relief. The modelling of the hair has been left fairly free, but there is more detail in the nearer parts. On a younger face the skin would have been left smoother, but still straight from the chisel so as to enliven the surface. Although the original photographs showed far more detail in the clothing, the forms have been simplified; only the parts considered essential to the composition have been included

Eyes cause problems, largely because people do not appreciate the spherical shape of the eyeball, how far back the outside corners are on the side of the face, and – particularly in relief – that the side view of the eye is quite different from the front (unless you are an ancient Egyptian). The eyeball pushes out the flesh of the eyebrow and the cheek.

The ear grows out of the back of the jaw line. I kept the ear surface parallel with the background, to maintain an angle with the side of the head.

Although the jaw has a hard shadow, it does not form a sharp line with the neck, so I used a veiner instead of stabbing down against it. The clothing, on the other hand, does meet the throat at a sharp angle. The mouth is also separated from the cheek by a deep shadow which should be carved with a veiner. The lips can be stabbed or chased in as the surface is pushed back, but the subtlety of the corner should be closely observed, especially the slope of the side of the lower lip and the diagonal hollow across the top lip.

Hair may be treated in many ways. It has thickness, and even in apparently straight hair there are locks (Fig 10.33). It should never look like a bathing cap or a ploughed field, unless deliberately stylized.

Making the relief appear deeper than it is

A successful relief appears to be deeper than it is. As a relief head is composed of curves, you can suggest depth by representing an evenly curved surface as a long, flat curve followed by a quickening turn down to the next level. This can be seen on the top and back of the present head as it approaches the ground. You may even give the illusion of greater depth by *minimal* undercutting (Fig 10.34).

The carver not only chooses the depth of relief, but also can experiment with surface treatment. It is always most important to remember that what you are making, even when it is a copy in the round of some natural object, is not the actual object but a sculpture of it in another material. The reasonable viewer accepts this, and even the least sympathetic is compelled to realize it when looking at relief.

FIG 10.34 An edge view of the completed relief, showing how much smaller the further (right) eye is, and the way the lines of brows and mouth would converge somewhere to the left of the viewer. Perspective rules, even in so short a distance. This view of the relief shows that the left shoulder is at the original surface of the wood, which was left flat. Modelling it would not add anything useful to the head. The quickness of the turn of the hair on top of the head down to the ground after the gentle curve of the side enhances the illusion of depth

CONCLUSION

You may use the human form in carving for its own sake, or you may use it, like life drawing, as a means of learning the wonderful possibilities of form, the effects of underlying structures and the kinds of shape and proportion that mankind feels most comfortable with. Whatever your prime reason, the figure should be a most exciting and rewarding subject for you, the artist craftsman.

Many carvers, especially when they first embark on figure work, concentrate on the conventionally pretty or sentimental forms: the idealized young woman or man, the child with a tear in its eye or its thumb in its mouth. You probably can make your fortune with these subjects, even if you do not do them particularly well. If you cannot see anything wrong with them, you may be sure that there are many, many people out there who will see nothing wrong with them either. However, being serious about your carving and having an urge to explore and develop, you will soon find that you are embarked on a journey of discovery that can go in an infinite number of directions and that has no end. You will learn to value the great variety of human types and to see beauty in the forms of a very fat model or in an ancient, wrinkled face or gnarled hand. Tragedy and pain may also move you to create.

You may go even further and simplify or stylize the figure, or even take parts of the human anatomy, internal or external, and turn them into abstract patterns or place them in strange juxtapositions, revelling in or merely exploring the shapes.

My final remarks are relevant whatever you choose to carve. Do everything with the excitement of exploration and creation. Try to feel in yourself something of the emotion or sense of movement that you wish the carving to convey. You can then be sure that, even if your technique and understanding are not fully fledged, you will produce something original, worthwhile and, possibly, powerful and moving.

It is natural when you begin carving to want to show your work to others. You need reassurance, and you will probably get it; but if you are an artist you will soon be making carvings because this is what you want to do, what you need to do. The opinion of others is only important if you need to sell in order to live. However, what you will find is that, if you are true to yourself and do not simply make what *you* think others want to see, you will have more self-respect and your carvings will, as your understanding and skill grow, have a magic to which the outside world will willingly respond.

GLOSSARY OF ANATOMICAL TERMS

acetabulum the socket in the pelvis which receives the head of the **femur**

Achilles tendon the tendon connecting the calf muscles to the heelbone

acromion the outer edge of the spine of the **scapula**

adductor any muscle which pulls part of the body towards the centre line

anterior forward

antihelix the curving fold just inside the outer margin of the ear

antitragus the upper boundary of the earlobe

aponeurosis a flattened sheet of tendon-like tissue

astragalus another name for the **talus**

atlas the uppermost **vertebra**, to which the skull is articulated

auricular cartilage the fleshy tube which joins the outer part of the ear to the head

biceps the muscle that flexes the forearm (**biceps brachii**), or the corresponding muscle in the leg (**biceps femoris**)

buccinator a muscle which compresses the cheek

carpals the eight bones which make up the wrist

carpal tunnel or **carpal ligament** the **fascia tissue** which holds in the tendons travelling through the wrist

clavicle the collarbone

coccyx the vestigial tail at the lower end of the human spinal column, comprising three, four or even five fused **vertebrae**

condyle either of the two knob-like projections at the lower end of the **femur**

coracoid process a forward projection towards the outer end of the **scapula**

cranium the part of the skull which contains the brain

deltoid the muscle which raises the arm and forms the outer surface of the shoulder

epicanthal fold a fold of skin over the inner corner (canthus) of the eye, characteristic of Mongolian peoples

epicondyles the protuberances at the lower end of the **humerus** which form part of the elbow joint

extensor a muscle used in straightening a joint

external auditory meatus the ear opening in the skull

external oblique muscle a wide muscle which extends from the **iliac crest** to the lower eight ribs

fascia tissue fibrous connective tissue which forms partitions between groups of muscles

femur the thighbone

fibula the outer and smaller of the two lower leg bones

flexor a muscle used in bending a joint

flexor carpi radialis a muscle of the forearm, whose tendon is prominent on the inside of the wrist

frontalis the large, flat muscle running down the forehead to the bridge of the nose

gastrocnemius the large muscle at the top of the calf

gluteus maximus   the principal muscle of the buttocks

gluteus medius   the fan-shaped muscle on the outside of the hip

great trochanter   the outer head of the thighbone

helix   the curving outer margin of the ear

humerus   the upper arm bone

iliac crest   the upper edge of the pelvis

iliac spine   any of the other edges of the pelvis

iliotibial band   a band of **fascia tissue** running the whole length of the outside of the thigh

intervertebral discs   the shock-absorbing discs of cartilage between the **vertebrae**

latissimus dorsi   the very wide muscle which runs from the top of the **humerus** to the lower part of the spine and the **iliac crest**

levatores labii superioris   two muscles which raise the upper lip, one of which also raises the wing of the nostril

lumbar region   the part of the spine between the lowest ribs and the pelvis

malleoli   the bony **processes** at the lower end of the **tibia** (**inner malleolus**) and **fibula** (**outer malleolus**), loosely known as 'anklebones'

mandible   the lower jawbone

masseter   a cheek muscle which moves the lower jaw

mastoid   a **process** at the bottom edge of the skull, just behind the lower jaw

maxilla   the upper jawbone

metacarpals   the five long bones between the **carpals** and the fingers

metatarsals   the five long bones between the **tarsals** and the toes

occiput   the hindmost part of the skull

olecranon   the 'funny bone' – the projection at the upper end of the **ulna** to which is attached the lowest tendon of the **triceps** of the arm

orbicularis oculi   the elliptical muscle which surrounds the eye

orbicularis oris   the elliptical muscle surrounding the mouth

orbit   the eye socket

os calcis, **os calcaneus** or **calcaneum**   the heelbone

patella   the kneecap

pectoral muscle   a large, plate-like muscle which runs from the inner part of the **clavicle** and the **sternum** to the **humerus**

peroneus   a calf muscle which allows the foot to turn outwards

phalanges   the individual bones forming the toes and fingers

philtrum   the groove running down from the **septum** of the nose to the middle of the top lip

pisiform carpal   the 'pea-shaped' **carpal** at the base of the little finger

popliteal fossa   the hollow between the tendons at the back of the knee

posterior   rearward

Poupart's ligament   the ligament which runs from the anterior superior **iliac spine** to the **symphysis pubis**, and forms the curved furrow between the abdomen and the thigh

process   any projection on the surface of a bone

pyramidalis   the muscle which runs down the centre of the forehead

radius   the outer of the two lower arm bones

ramus   the wing of the lower jaw, to which the **temporal muscle** is attached

rectus abdominis   an oblong muscle running from the arch at the bottom of the **thorax** down to **Poupart's ligament**

rectus femoris   the **extensor** which runs down the centre of the front of the thigh

sacrospinalis   a muscle which runs beside the spine from the **sacrum** and underlies the **aponeurosis** of the **latissimus dorsi**

sacrum the part of the backbone attached to the pelvis, comprising five fused **vertebrae**

sartorius the long, thin muscle which runs diagonally across the front of the thigh from the anterior superior spine of the pelvis to the inside of the knee

scapula the shoulder blade

septum the partition between the nostrils

serratus magnus or **serratus anterior** a wide muscle which anchors the **scapula** to the ribs

solar plexus the network of nerves supplying the abdominal organs

soleus a muscle of the calf, partly overlaid by the **gastrocnemius**

spinal column the spine or backbone

steatopygy an accumulation of fat on the buttocks, characteristic of certain racial groups

sterno-cleido-mastoid the muscle that runs from the **mastoid process** around the windpipe to the top of the **sternum** and the inside of the **clavicle**

sternum the breastbone

styloid processes the projections at the lower end of the **radius** and **ulna**, forming part of the wrist joint

superior upper

supraorbital notch a small indentation in the middle of the upper edge of the eye socket

sutures the interlocking joints or seams between the bones of the skull

symphysis pubis the part of the pelvis behind the genitals, to which some of the leg muscles are attached

talus the uppermost bone of the foot, which articulates with the leg; it is the anklebone proper, and is not visible on the surface

tarsals the seven bones which make up the main body of the foot

temporal muscle the fan-shaped muscle, attached to the temples, which closes the lower jaw

tensor fasciae latae the muscle attaching the **iliotibial band** to the pelvis at the front

thorax the ribcage

tibia the inner and larger of the two lower leg bones, the shinbone

tibialis anticus or **tibialis anterior** the muscle which runs from the head of the **fibula** down to the ankle

tragus the small fleshy projection on the cheek immediately in front of the ear hole

trapezius the large, flat, triangular muscle extending from the base of the **occiput** to the shoulder and down to the middle of the back on each side

triceps the muscle which extends the forearm

ulna the inner of the two lower arm bones

vertebrae the articulated segments which form the **spinal column**

zygomatic arch the narrow ridge of bone that runs back from the cheekbone at the bottom outside corner of the eye socket to just in front of the ear hole

FURTHER READING

Rhys Carpenter, *Greek Sculpture: A Critical Review* (Chicago University Press, 1960)

John Cody, *Atlas of Foreshortening: The Human Figure in Deep Perspective* (New York: Van Nostrand Reinhold, 1984)

Eliot Goldfinger, *Human Anatomy for Artists* (Oxford University Press, 1991)

Edouard Lanteri, *Modelling and Sculpting the Human Figure* (repr. New York: Dover, 1985)

Eadweard Muybridge, *The Male and Female Figure in Motion* (repr. New York: Dover, 1984)

Fritz Schider, *An Atlas of Anatomy For Artists,* 3rd edn. (New York: Dover, 1957)

András Szunyohgy and György Fehér, *Anatomy Drawing School* (Cologne: Könemann, 1996)

Eugene Wolff with George Charlton, *Anatomy for Artists*, 4th edn. (London: H. K. Lewis & Co., 1962)

ABOUT THE AUTHOR

Dick Onians, born in 1940 in a house full of books, folk carvings and other sculpture, spent his childhood climbing trees, reading and whittling. He read Classics and English at Cambridge, took his PGCE at London University and taught English and Latin at Dudley Boys' Grammar School for three years. He then studied Woodcarving at the City and Guilds of London Art School under the late William Wheeler. From 1968 he taught English and sculpture part-time while establishing himself as a sculptor in wood and stone. In 1978 he returned to the City and Guilds Art School to teach part-time on its unique courses in traditional wood and stone carving. He is now Senior Woodcarving Tutor there. In 1992 he pioneered the formal part-time Creative Studies course in woodcarving for the City and Guilds Institute, which he teaches at Missenden Abbey, Buckinghamshire.

He also teaches at many other colleges near his home in Hertfordshire and around Britain. He is a regular contributor to *Woodcarving* magazine and is an Associate of the Royal Society of British

Photograph: Oppi Pillai

Sculptors. Although versatile as a sculptor, he prefers to carve his own abstract shapes in wood and stone. He has exhibited widely in one-man and group exhibitions, and his work is in private collections around the world.

His first book, *Essential Woodcarving Techniques*, was published by GMC Publications in 1997.

INDEX

GMC Publications

BOOKS

WOODCARVING

The Art of the Woodcarver	GMC Publications
Carving Architectural Detail in Wood: The Classical Tradition	Frederick Wilbur
Carving Birds & Beasts	GMC Publications
Carving the Human Figure: Studies in Wood and Stone	Dick Onians
Carving Nature: Wildlife Studies in Wood	Frank Fox-Wilson
Carving Realistic Birds	David Tippey
Decorative Woodcarving	Jeremy Williams
Elements of Woodcarving	Chris Pye
Essential Woodcarving Techniques	Dick Onians
Further Useful Tips for Woodcarvers	GMC Publications
Lettercarving in Wood: A Practical Course	Chris Pye
Making & Using Working Drawings for Realistic Model Animals	Basil F. Fordham
Power Tools for Woodcarving	David Tippey
Practical Tips for Turners & Carvers	GMC Publications
Relief Carving in Wood: A Practical Introduction	Chris Pye
Understanding Woodcarving	GMC Publications
Understanding Woodcarving in the Round	GMC Publications
Useful Techniques for Woodcarvers	GMC Publications
Wildfowl Carving – Volume 1	Jim Pearce
Wildfowl Carving – Volume 2	Jim Pearce
Woodcarving: A Complete Course	Ron Butterfield
Woodcarving: A Foundation Course	Zoë Gertner
Woodcarving for Beginners	GMC Publications
Woodcarving Tools & Equipment Test Reports	GMC Publications
Woodcarving Tools, Materials & Equipment	Chris Pye

WOODTURNING

Adventures in Woodturning	David Springett
Bert Marsh: Woodturner	Bert Marsh
Bowl Turning Techniques Masterclass	Tony Boase
Colouring Techniques for Woodturners	Jan Sanders
Contemporary Turned Wood: New Perspectives in a Rich Tradition	Ray Leier, Jan Peters & Kevin Wallace
The Craftsman Woodturner	Peter Child
Decorative Techniques for Woodturners	Hilary Bowen
Fun at the Lathe	R.C. Bell
Illustrated Woodturning Techniques	John Hunnex
Intermediate Woodturning Projects	GMC Publications
Keith Rowley's Woodturning Projects	Keith Rowley
Practical Tips for Turners & Carvers	GMC Publications
Turning Green Wood	Michael O'Donnell
Turning Miniatures in Wood	John Sainsbury
Turning Pens and Pencils	Kip Christensen & Rex Burningham
Understanding Woodturning	Ann & Bob Phillips
Useful Techniques for Woodturners	GMC Publications
Useful Woodturning Projects	GMC Publications
Woodturning: Bowls, Platters, Hollow Forms, Vases, Vessels, Bottles, Flasks, Tankards, Plates	GMC Publications
Woodturning: A Foundation Course (New Edition)	Keith Rowley
Woodturning: A Fresh Approach	Robert Chapman
Woodturning: An Individual Approach	Dave Regester
Woodturning: A Source Book of Shapes	John Hunnex
Woodturning Jewellery	Hilary Bowen
Woodturning Masterclass	Tony Boase
Woodturning Techniques	GMC Publications
Woodturning Tools & Equipment Test Reports	GMC Publications
Woodturning Wizardry	David Springett

WOODWORKING

Advanced Scrollsaw Projects	GMC Publications
Bird Boxes and Feeders for the Garden	Dave Mackenzie
Complete Woodfinishing	Ian Hosker
David Charlesworth's Furniture-Making Techniques	David Charlesworth
The Encyclopedia of Joint Making	Terrie Noll
Furniture & Cabinetmaking Projects	GMC Publications
Furniture-Making Projects for the Wood Craftsman	GMC Publications
Furniture-Making Techniques for the Wood Craftsman	GMC Publications
Furniture Projects	Rod Wales
Furniture Restoration (Practical Crafts)	Kevin Jan Bonner
Furniture Restoration and Repair for Beginners	Kevin Jan Bonner
Furniture Restoration Workshop	Kevin Jan Bonner
Green Woodwork	Mike Abbott
Kevin Ley's Furniture Projects	Kevin Ley
Making & Modifying Woodworking Tools	Jim Kingshott
Making Chairs and Tables	GMC Publications
Making Classic English Furniture	Paul Richardson
Making Little Boxes from Wood	John Bennett
Making Screw Threads in Wood	Fred Holder
Making Shaker Furniture	Barry Jackson
Making Woodwork Aids and Devices	Robert Wearing
Mastering the Router	Ron Fox
Minidrill: Fifteen Projects	John Everett
Pine Furniture Projects for the Home	Dave Mackenzie
Practical Scrollsaw Patterns	John Everett
Router Magic: Jigs, Fixtures and Tricks to Unleash your Router's Full Potential	Bill Hylton
Routing for Beginners	Anthony Bailey
The Scrollsaw: Twenty Projects	John Everett
Sharpening: The Complete Guide	Jim Kingshott
Sharpening Pocket Reference Book	Jim Kingshott
Simple Scrollsaw Projects	GMC Publications
Space-Saving Furniture Projects	Dave Mackenzie
Stickmaking: A Complete Course	Andrew Jones & Clive George
Stickmaking Handbook	Andrew Jones & Clive George
Test Reports: The Router and Furniture & Cabinetmaking	GMC Publications
Veneering: A Complete Course	Ian Hosker
Veneering Handbook	Ian Hosker
Woodfinishing Handbook (Practical Crafts)	Ian Hosker
Woodworking with the Router: Professional Router Techniques any Woodworker can Use	Bill Hylton & Fred Matlack
The Workshop	Jim Kingshott

UPHOLSTERY

The Upholsterer's Pocket Reference Book	David James
Upholstery: A Complete Course (Revised Edition)	David James
Upholstery Restoration	David James
Upholstery Techniques & Projects	David James
Upholstery Tips and Hints	David James

TOYMAKING

Designing & Making Wooden Toys — *Terry Kelly*
Fun to Make Wooden Toys & Games — *Jeff & Jennie Loader*
Restoring Rocking Horses — *Clive Green & Anthony Dew*
Scrollsaw Toy Projects — *Ivor Carlyle*
Scrollsaw Toys for All Ages — *Ivor Carlyle*
Wooden Toy Projects — *GMC Publications*

DOLLS' HOUSES AND MINIATURES

1/12 Scale Character Figures for the Dolls' House — *James Carrington*
Architecture for Dolls' Houses — *Joyce Percival*
The Authentic Georgian Dolls' House — *Brian Long*
A Beginners' Guide to the Dolls' House Hobby — *Jean Nisbett*
Celtic, Medieval and Tudor Wall Hangings in
 1/12 Scale Needlepoint — *Sandra Whitehead*
The Complete Dolls' House Book — *Jean Nisbett*
The Dolls' House 1/24 Scale: A Complete Introduction — *Jean Nisbett*
Dolls' House Accessories, Fixtures and Fittings — *Andrea Barham*
Dolls' House Bathrooms: Lots of Little Loos — *Patricia King*
Dolls' House Fireplaces and Stoves — *Patricia King*
Dolls' House Window Treatments — *Eve Harwood*
Easy to Make Dolls' House Accessories — *Andrea Barham*
Heraldic Miniature Knights — *Peter Greenhill*
How to Make Your Dolls' House Special:
 Fresh Ideas for Decorating — *Beryl Armstrong*
Make Your Own Dolls' House Furniture — *Maurice Harper*
Making Dolls' House Furniture — *Patricia King*
Making Georgian Dolls' Houses — *Derek Rowbottom*
Making Miniature Food and Market Stalls — *Angie Scarr*
Making Miniature Gardens — *Freida Gray*
Making Miniature Oriental Rugs & Carpets — *Meik & Ian McNaughton*
Making Period Dolls' House Accessories — *Andrea Barham*
Making Tudor Dolls' Houses — *Derek Rowbottom*
Making Victorian Dolls' House Furniture — *Patricia King*
Miniature Bobbin Lace — *Roz Snowden*
Miniature Embroidery for the Georgian Dolls' House — *Pamela Warner*
Miniature Embroidery for the Victorian Dolls' House — *Pamela Warner*
Miniature Needlepoint Carpets — *Janet Granger*
More Miniature Oriental Rugs & Carpets — *Meik & Ian McNaughton*
Needlepoint 1/12 Scale: Design Collections for the Dolls' House — *Felicity Price*
The Secrets of the Dolls' House Makers — *Jean Nisbett*

CRAFTS

American Patchwork Designs in Needlepoint — *Melanie Tacon*
A Beginners' Guide to Rubber Stamping — *Brenda Hunt*
Blackwork: A New Approach — *Brenda Day*
Celtic Cross Stitch Designs — *Carol Phillipson*
Celtic Knotwork Designs — *Sheila Sturrock*
Celtic Knotwork Handbook — *Sheila Sturrock*
Celtic Spirals and Other Designs — *Sheila Sturrock*
Collage from Seeds, Leaves and Flowers — *Joan Carver*
Complete Pyrography — *Stephen Poole*
Contemporary Smocking — *Dorothea Hall*
Creating Colour with Dylon — *Dylon International*
Creative Doughcraft — *Patricia Hughes*
Creative Embroidery Techniques
 Using Colour Through Gold — *Daphne J. Ashby & Jackie Woolsey*
The Creative Quilter: Techniques and Projects — *Pauline Brown*
Decorative Beaded Purses — *Enid Taylor*
Designing and Making Cards — *Glennis Gilruth*
Glass Engraving Pattern Book — *John Everett*

Glass Painting — *Emma Sedman*
Handcrafted Rugs — *Sandra Hardy*
How to Arrange Flowers: A Japanese Approach to English Design — *Taeko Marvelly*
How to Make First-Class Cards — *Debbie Brown*
An Introduction to Crewel Embroidery — *Mave Glenny*
Making and Using Working Drawings for Realistic Model Animals — *Basil F. Fordham*
Making Character Bears — *Valerie Tyler*
Making Decorative Screens — *Amanda Howes*
Making Fairies and Fantastical Creatures — *Julie Sharp*
Making Greetings Cards for Beginners — *Pat Sutherland*
Making Hand-Sewn Boxes: Techniques and Projects — *Jackie Woolsey*
Making Knitwear Fit — *Pat Ashforth & Steve Plummer*
Making Mini Cards, Gift Tags & Invitations — *Glennis Gilruth*
Making Soft-Bodied Dough Characters — *Patricia Hughes*
Natural Ideas for Christmas:
 Fantastic Decorations to Make — *Josie Cameron-Ashcroft & Carol Cox*
Needlepoint: A Foundation Course — *Sandra Hardy*
New Ideas for Crochet: Stylish Projects for the Home — *Darsha Capaldi*
Patchwork for Beginners — *Pauline Brown*
Pyrography Designs — *Norma Gregory*
Pyrography Handbook (Practical Crafts) — *Stephen Poole*
Ribbons and Roses — *Lee Lockheed*
Rose Windows for Quilters — *Angela Besley*
Rubber Stamping with Other Crafts — *Lynne Garner*
Sponge Painting — *Ann Rooney*
Stained Glass: Techniques and Projects — *Mary Shanahan*
Step-by-Step Pyrography Projects for the Solid Point Machine — *Norma Gregory*
Tassel Making for Beginners — *Enid Taylor*
Tatting Collage — *Lindsay Rogers*
Temari: A Traditional Japanese Embroidery Technique — *Margaret Ludlow*
Theatre Models in Paper and Card — *Robert Burgess*
Trip Around the World: 25 Patchwork, Quilting
 and Appliqué Projects — *Gail Lawther*
Trompe l'Oeil: Techniques and Projects — *Jan Lee Johnson*
Wool Embroidery and Design — *Lee Lockheed*

GARDENING

Auriculas for Everyone: How to Grow and Show Perfect Plants — *Mary Robinson*
Beginners' Guide to Herb Gardening — *Yvonne Cuthbertson*
Bird Boxes and Feeders for the Garden — *Dave Mackenzie*
The Birdwatcher's Garden — *Hazel & Pamela Johnson*
Broad-Leaved Evergreens — *Stephen G. Haw*
Companions to Clematis: Growing Clematis with Other Plants — *Marigold Badcock*
Creating Contrast with Dark Plants — *Freya Martin*
Creating Small Habitats for Wildlife in your Garden — *Josie Briggs*
Gardening with Wild Plants — *Julian Slatcher*
Growing Cacti and Other Succulents in the
 Conservatory and Indoors — *Shirley-Anne Bell*
Growing Cacti and Other Succulents in the Garden — *Shirley Anne Bell*
Hardy Perennials: A Beginner's Guide — *Eric Sawford*
The Living Tropical Greenhouse:
 Creating a Haven for Butterflies — *John & Maureen Tampion*
Orchids are Easy: A Beginner's Guide to their Care and Cultivation — *Tom Gilland*
Plant Alert: A Garden Guide for Parents — *Catherine Collins*
Planting Plans for Your Garden — *Jenny Shukman*
Plants that Span the Seasons — *Roger Wilson*
Sink and Container Gardening Using Dwarf Hardy Plants — *Chris & Valerie Wheeler*

PHOTOGRAPHY

An Essential Guide to Bird Photography — *Steve Young*
Light in the Landscape: A Photographer's Year — *Peter Watson*

VIDEOS

Drop-in and Pinstuffed Seats	*David James*
Stuffover Upholstery	*David James*
Elliptical Turning	*David Springett*
Woodturning Wizardry	*David Springett*
Turning Between Centres: The Basics	*Dennis White*
Turning Bowls	*Dennis White*
Boxes, Goblets and Screw Threads	*Dennis White*
Novelties and Projects	*Dennis White*
Classic Profiles	*Dennis White*
Twists and Advanced Turning	*Dennis White*
Sharpening the Professional Way	*Jim Kingshott*
Sharpening Turning & Carving Tools	*Jim Kingshott*
Bowl Turning	*John Jordan*
Hollow Turning	*John Jordan*
Woodturning: A Foundation Course	*Keith Rowley*
Carving a Figure: The Female Form	*Ray Gonzalez*
The Router: A Beginner's Guide	*Alan Goodsell*
The Scroll Saw: A Beginner's Guide	*John Burke*

MAGAZINES

WOODTURNING · WOODCARVING · FURNITURE & CABINETMAKING
THE ROUTER · WOODWORKING
THE DOLLS' HOUSE MAGAZINE
WATER GARDENING · EXOTIC GARDENING · GARDEN CALENDAR
OUTDOOR PHOTOGRAPHY · BLACK & WHITE PHOTOGRAPHY
BUSINESSMATTERS

The above represents a full list of all titles currently published or scheduled to be published.
All are available direct from the Publishers or through bookshops, newsagents and specialist retailers.
To place an order, or to obtain a complete catalogue, contact:

GMC Publications,
Castle Place, 166 High Street, Lewes, East Sussex BN7 1XU, United Kingdom
Tel: 01273 488005 Fax: 01273 478606
E-mail: pubs@thegmcgroup.com

Orders by credit card are accepted